# CAPITOL CRIME

# CAPITOL CRIME

WASHINGTON'S COVER-UP OF THE KILLING OF MIRIAM CAREY

★ ★ ★ ★ ★

## GARTH KANT

 WND Books

# CAPITOL CRIME

Published by WND Books, Washington, D.C. WND Books is a registered trademark of WorldNetDaily.com, Inc. ("WND")

Book designed by Mark Karis
Cover photo by Linda Davidson / *The Washington Post* via Getty Images

WND Books are available at special discounts for bulk purchases. WND Books also publishes books in electronic formats. For more information call (541) 474-1776, e-mail orders@wndbooks.com, or visit www.wndbooks.com.

Paperback ISBN: 978-1-944229-27-6
eBook ISBN: 978-1-944229-28-3

Library of Congress Cataloging-in-Publication Data
Names: Kant, Garth, author.
Title: Capitol crime : Washington's cover-up of the killing of Miriam Carey / Garth Kant.
Description: Washington, D.C. : WND Books, [2016] | Includes bibliographical references and index.
Identifiers: LCCN 2016015931 (print) | LCCN 2016025757 (ebook) | ISBN 9781944229276 (hardcover) | ISBN 9781944229283 (e-book)
Subjects: LCSH: Carey, Miriam, -2013. | Police shootings--Washington (D.C.)--Case studies. | Murder--Washington (D.C.)--Case studies.
Classification: LCC HV6534.W3 K36 2016 (print) | LCC HV6534.W3 (ebook) | DDC 364.1/32--dc23
LC record available at https://lccn.loc.gov/2016015931

*Printed in the United States of America*
16 17 18 19 20 21 LBM 9 8 7 6 5 4 3 2 1

*This book is dedicated to my mother, Sheila, her husband, Tim, my father, Hal, his wife, Jesse, and my brothers, Tony and Jonas.*

# CONTENTS

# PREFACE

A TWIST OF FATE put me on a long and exhaustive quest to get to the bottom of the Carey case.

Through sheer happenstance, I was one of the first reporters to arrive on the scene of big, breaking news, the Capitol Hill shooting of October 3, 2013.

I had just finished up a story at the U.S. District Court at Third Street and Constitution Avenue, when, seemingly, every squad car in the city went screaming by the cafeteria window facing the Capitol.

The flashing lights all converged on a spot about two blocks up Constitution, near the Capitol.

A quick Internet search for "Capitol Hill" turned up a one-sentence story that shots had been fired. Local media had most likely picked that up from police scanners, and it appeared no one was yet reporting from the scene.

I hustled down the street, took a few quick pictures as I approached the police line, and sent them to my editors. The situation looked ominous.

An ambulance and a badly mangled police car were in the

middle of the road. Another ambulance was just leaving with siren blaring.

Police had traffic on Constitution blocked off at Louisiana Avenue, all the way up to the Capitol. Gawkers lined both sides of the street.

An open-air truck carrying soldiers armed to the teeth drove by. This did not look good.

WND photo by Garth Kant.

I realized I would learn nothing by standing among the crowd of onlookers, so I walked toward the Capitol in search of someone who knew anything.

I found a pair of eyewitnesses who had heard rapid-fire gunshots and seen a police chase go from Garfield Circle at the edge of the Capitol Hill west lawn up Constitution.

I called my assignment editor and played the interview audio to him over the phone so he could publish the eyewitness accounts as soon as possible.

Police then began clearing the Capitol's west lawn. I asked an officer if there was an ongoing threat and he told me a suspect was "down."

"Dead?"

Just down, was all he knew, so I phoned that in.

As we were shepherded to the other side of Constitution, I asked another officer if a PIO (public information officer) would be speaking to the press. He said yes and pointed to the area where they were herding us.

While waiting, I did what every other reporter was doing: asking if anybody knew anything more. No one did.

Shots were fired, but by whom? Police? The driver? Was anyone hurt? Was anyone dead? Was it terrorism?

After a while, a rumor emerged that the driver was a woman. And there may have been a baby involved.

A baby?

The news conference looked like a hundred lions surrounding a zebra.

Press waiting for a police statement. WND photo by Garth Kant.

barricade, and after "shots were potentially fired" officers pursued the vehicle in a high-speed chase. They would later say the driver hit an officer with her car.[1]

None of that would turn out to be true.

By the next day, I noticed things were not adding up.

Why had police taken such radical and lethal action against what turned out to be a suburban mother with a baby—but no gun?

By the time this book went to press, I had written thirty-nine investigative stories on the Carey case. WND has published more than eighty stories on Carey.

The story had begun as an apparent terrorism threat in the nation's capital that gripped the city, the country, and the entire world with overwhelming wall-to-wall media coverage. When it ended as the highly questionable shooting of an unarmed woman by federal officers for the simple mistake of making a wrong turn, the media virtually ignored the truth.

With the exception of WND.

CEO Joseph Farah implored me to stay on the story, and that's precisely what I did.

First, I obtained the initial police report on the incident, in the form of an affidavit, from the Carey family attorney. This is when disturbing discrepancies first came to light.[2]

The report revealed that Carey never rammed a White House gate but had merely tried to drive around a bike rack. Furthermore, officers had not tried to stop Carey from entering the post but from leaving it. The report gave no explanation as to why officers pursued Carey. Or why they shot her.

The officers involved in the incident were members of the U.S. Capitol Police and the Uniformed Division of the U.S. Secret Service. The investigation was done by the Washington,

United States District Court
For the
District of Columbia

AFFIDAVIT IN SUPPORT OF A SEARCH WA

Case 1: 13-mj-744
Assigned to: Magistrate Judge Deborah A. Robinson
Assigned Date: 10/4/2013
Description: Search and Seizure Warrant

FOR THE ENTIRE VEHICLE, INFINITY, G37XS, VEHICLE IDENTIFICATION NUMBER
(VIN#) JN1CV6EL413M261683, CONNECTICUT LICENSE # 323-YNS. THE VEHICLE IS
DESCRIBED AS A TWO (2) DOOR, BLACK COLORED, 2010 NISSAN INFINITI LT.

**RESUME:** Your affiant is a sworn member of the Metropolitan Police Department, assigned
to the Internal Affairs Bureau (IAB), Internal Affairs Division (IAD), and has been so
employed for more than (19) nineteen years.

Your affiant is currently assigned to the Internal Affairs Division (IAD). Your affiant has
investigated a variety of criminal offenses. She has arrested and assisted in arresting
numerous subjects for various offenses, and assisted with the preparation and execution of
numerous search warrants.

**POLICE REPORT:** On Thursday, October 3, 2013, Detectives of the Metropolitan Police
Department's Internal Affairs Division, became involved in the investigation of a police
involved shooting.

This incident began on Thursday, October 3, 2013, at approximately 2:18 p.m. at a vehicle
checkpoint to the White House, located at 15th and E Street, Northwest, Washington, D.C.
Members of the United States Secret Service, Uniformed Division, (hereinafter, "USSS-
UD), encountered the aforementioned vehicle at 15th and E Streets Northwest, Washington
D.C.. The suspect vehicle was being operated by a black female (hereinafter, "Decedent").
Decedent refused to stop at the vehicle checkpoint and made a U-turn and began to flee in
the vehicle. A USSS-UD officer attempted to block the vehicle with a bicycle rack,
however, the vehicle pushed over the bicycle rack, knocking the officer to the ground.

Officers from the USSS-UD initiated a pursuit of the suspect vehicle. Decedent was
observed operating the vehicle erratically, violating several District of Columbia traffic
regulations. Decedent entered a traffic circle against the flow of traffic and drove onto a
curb in front of #10 Maryland Avenue, Southwest, Washington DC. The suspect
vehicle was immediately surrounded by officers from the USSS-UD, and United States
Capitol Police (hereinafter, "USCP"). Decedent then drove the suspect vehicle in
reverse, striking a USSS-UD police vehicle. Members from both USSS-UD and USCP
then discharged their service weapons at the vehicle. Decedent then drove the suspect
vehicle off the curb, traveling northbound on First Street, Northeast and then eastbound
in the 100 block of Constitution Avenue, Northeast, Washington, D.C. Officers from
USSS-UD and USCP pursued the suspect vehicle to 2nd Street and Constitution
Avenue, Northeast where Decedent stopped the suspect vehicle abruptly, and then

1

D.C., Metropolitan Police Department, or MPD. Its report
was reviewed by the office of the U.S. Attorney for Washington,
D.C., a branch of the Justice Department.

I filed a FOIA (Freedom of Information Act) request in

turned left and drove over a median strip. Decedent then drove in reverse in the 200 block of Maryland Avenue, Northeast, where Decedent again refused to stop.

At this point, officers from both USSS-UD and USCP fired several rounds into the suspect vehicle, striking Decedent. The vehicle came to rest on the median area directly behind the guard's booth on the United States Capitol grounds.

Decedent, along with an uninjured child, were removed from the vehicle. Decedent was transported to the Washington Hospital Center where she was pronounced dead by Dr. Christine Trankiem of the medical staff. Decedent's remains were transported to the Office of the Chief Medical Examiner for the District of Columbia pending an autopsy.

The suspect vehicle was recovered as evidence and has remained in police custody. Based on the above facts and circumstances, your affiant believes that the vehicle described above is of evidentiary value and may contain physical evidence such as expended bullets or bullet fragments fired by the officers; vehicle ownership paperwork; maps, documents, and/or photographs of, or pertaining to, the White House; alcohol or drugs (legal or illegal); and/or evidence of a mechanical malfunction or lack thereof may be inside the suspect vehicle.

Your affiant respectfully requests that a District Court Search Warrant be issued for the entire vehicle known as a 2010 Nissan Infiniti G37XS, VIN#JN1CV6EL413M261683, Connecticut License # 323-YNS.

Felicia Laucen, Lt. MPD

_____          _____  10/4/13
Affiant                           United States Attorney

                                          OCT - 4 2013
_____
Subscribed and sworn to before me this_____day of_____2013

Magistrate
United States District Court
DEBORAH A. ROBINSON
U.S MAGISTRATE JUDGE

2

early 2014 with the MPD for the forensics report and surveil-lance video footage but was denied. Police refused to release any evidence or additional reports, citing an ongoing investigation. The investigation then dragged on for months.

On July 10, 2014, the Justice Department announced the completion of the investigation and said no charges would be filed against the officers. I then made a FOIA request on August 4, 2014, with MPD, requesting "all materials used in the investigation into the October 3, 2013, fatal shooting of Miriam Carey, by uniformed agents of the U.S. Secret Service, and officers of the U.S. Capitol Police Department, to include the final report and findings of that investigation."

That request was denied on October 17, 2014.

Not wanting to submit to a stonewall, I drafted a letter of appeal and sent it to Washington, DC, mayor Vincent Gray. On April 4, 2015, the associate director of the Mayor's Office of Legal Counsel called to inform me that the FOIA appeal would be granted and I could pick up the material requested from the Metro Police headquarters.[3]

The only redactions were supposed to be the names of witnesses, out of concern for privacy. In fact, the report was heavily redacted, including entire pages. Much evidence was omitted. There was no video. Or photographs. Dozens of witness statements were missing, as were officer statements. In the material I did have, I discovered there were many more serious discrepancies between what witnesses reported and the official version of events. Most notably, not one witness reported that Carey was driving at officers when they shot her dead, even though they had claimed they'd shot in self-defense both at Garfield Circle and at the final scene on Constitution Ave.

After reviewing the material, I wrote a five-part series for WND on what I'd found.

I had also filed a FOIA request for the complete investigation and findings with the Justice Department on August 4, 2014:

I am filing this FOIA request to obtain all materials used in the investigation by the Washington, D.C. Metropolitan Police Department, and reviewed by the U.S. Attorney's Office for the District of Columbia, into the October, 3, 2013 fatal shooting of Miriam Carey by uniformed agents of the U.S. Secret Service and officers of the U.S. Capitol Police Department. I am also requesting the final report and findings of that investigation.

By law the Justice Department was supposed to respond within twenty days. After months of futile inquiries, however, I was informed on March 19, 2015, that the request was waiting to be assigned and processed by a paralegal and that I was "welcome to check on the status within a few weeks."

Instead, my employer, WND, and I enlisted the help of the government-watchdog group Judicial Watch, and on April 14, 2015, we sued the Justice Department.

The Justice Department agreed to comply with the FOIA request and began producing a series of documents on September 9, 2015.[4]

And, once again, the material provided was incomplete.

Significantly, still missing was surveillance video of Carey's entry and departure at the White House guard post and her shooting death on Constitution, so there was still no evidence that showed exactly what happened to Carey. And there was still nothing that indicated that investigators had ever conducted an *analysis* of the evidence.

Or that they had even conducted an investigation.

It seemed clear that investigation of the investigators was in order. This book is a chronicle of that effort, which is still a work in progress.

This book couldn't be possible without support from a number of people. I thank my WND colleagues: Chelsea Schilling, my good friend and editor of the Carey stories as they appeared in WND, and bosses, David Kupelian (without whom I wouldn't have my job) and Joseph Farah (without whom there wouldn't be this book.) I'd also like to thank Carey family attorney Eric Sanders for his magnificent assistance and unflagging pursuit of the truth, and the dedicated and talented staff of Judicial Watch for their invaluable efforts in the legal arena.

Due to the extensive amount of material collected, we have set up a website documenting the Miriam Carey scandal. It includes the timeline of what happened, links to my featured stories about the scandal, an extensive list of related stories, the color photographs and images that are included in this book, related videos, and more. Go to go.wnd.com/miriamcarey/ to find out more.

# WHY DOES THE MIRIAM CAREY STORY MATTER?

ERICA WAS UTTERLY HELPLESS. Not yet old enough to talk. But she was a bright and observant child, with darting eyes, acutely aware of everything happening around her.

She was in the backseat, while driving was the one person around whom her whole life revolved, her mother. The person who provided everything—everything needed to stay alive. The one person who was her whole world.

It was a gorgeous, sun-drenched autumn day, and it would have been a long but pleasant drive.

Suddenly, a strange man was banging his hand on the back of the car. A behemoth of a man, his flushed face turning beet red, was blocking the way, dragging something big in front of the car.

Frenzied, angry men appeared from everywhere, and they were all yelling at Erica and her mom.

As her mother somehow managed to escape the confusion and drive away, even more alarming sounds began to pierce the air: wailing sirens, and they kept getting closer.

Then the scariest sounds of all—gunshots. Loud, horrific cannon blasts, to a child's ear.

She heard the bullets zing through the air and pierce the car's armor with the searing screeches of hot lead on metal.

Erica's entire world then caved in, as the window behind her suddenly exploded, shattering into a million pieces on top of her head. She was covered in glass and blood as her mother was shot numerous time in the back.

Then came the bullet that ended it all—into the left side of the back of her mother's head . . . as a crimson gusher came spurting from just behind her ear.

And it all happened right in front of the little girl's face. Etched into her eyes for eternity.

The bullet-ridden body slumped in her seat, the last glimpse Erica would ever have of her mother.

The noises started all over again, but by then she was numb.

People everywhere began yelling. A strange man smashed a window and pulled her out of the car. He put her in the arms of a strange woman. And Erica was whisked off to the sterile embrace of a hospital to receive urgent treatment for God-only-knows-what trauma.

She would never see her mother again.

Erica's last sight of her mother was her savage killing. She was just thirteen months old and drenched in her mother's blood.

How much would she remember?

How much could she forget?

She would never be the same. And neither would her world.

*****

Judging by the evidence, what you have just read is a reasonably accurate portrayal of little Erica Carey's experience on October 3, 2013, in the heart of the nation's capital.

No one knows why the toddler's mother, Miriam Carey, drove to Washington from their suburban Connecticut home that balmy autumn day. But it was a day that ended with the violent death of Erica's mother at the hands of elite federal police, and was shown on virtually every television screen in the country.

And Miriam would become the black life that didn't matter.

In today's America, the idea that black lives are too often unnecessarily ended by trigger-happy police has turned city after city upside down with angry and sometimes violent demonstrations and dominated the news media. Each time a black person is killed by police, the movement escalates. Some of the high-profile cases have been indeed troubling, like that of Eric Garner, whose repeated cries of "I can't breathe" became a rallying cry in the movement. Other cases, like that of Michael Brown (who never said, "Hands up, don't shoot" and turned out to be the aggressor), were shams—the products of lying "eyewitnesses" and what many feel were racial hucksters and a biased and lazy news media.

And yet, mysteriously, perhaps the most sensational and high-profile case of all, that of Miriam Carey—shot dead, toddler daughter in tow, by police in Washington, D.C., in the shadow of the Capitol and carried as breaking news around the world—magically disappeared from view after the initial media coverage, in which virtually every "fact" the press reported was dead wrong. To this day, there have been no demonstrations, no media interest, no "Black Lives Matter" marches. Just silence. Why?

Consider just the most basic facts in the Carey case:

She was shot in the back.

She was unarmed.

And police claimed they fired in self-defense.

That is what makes the Miriam Carey story unlike any other. It's a story that defies explanation.

First they said she was a terrorist. When that didn't turn out to be true, they said she was crazy. When that didn't turn out to be true either, the media dropped the story.

It took WND to set the record straight, and this book is the result of that long and detailed investigation.

When the official story just did not add up, the investigation was propelled by two basic questions: Why did they kill her? And how could no one care?

Consider the evidence. We, the public, were told this:

- Miriam Carey used her car to ram a White House gate.

- Officers tried to stop her from entering White House grounds.

- Shots may have been fired at the White House.

- Carey ran over an officer, fled the scene, and led police on a high-speed chase.

- Officers fired in self-defense.

- And officers did not know there was a toddler in the backseat of her car.

None of that turned out to be true. Here's what really happened:

- Carey was shot in the back.

- She was not carrying a weapon.

- She did not ram any gates.

- She did not try to enter the White House.

- She did not violate any laws.

- She did not flee, but left at a lawful speed.

- A Secret Service agent saw the child in her car before the chase.

- And, perhaps strangest of all, Secret Service agents did not try to stop her from entering a White House guard post—inexplicably, they tried to stop her from leaving.

What at first looked like a straightforward story of authorities stopping a deranged woman from trying to ram her way into the White House turned out to be, upon a closer look, anything but an open-and-shut case.

Why is this case important?

Famed civil libertarian Nat Hentoff contends that the evidence is strong that authorities recklessly killed Carey and that the officers involved and their superiors must be held to account for her death for the sake of the country.

"This is a classic case of police out of control and, therefore, guilty of plain murder," he said in discussion with the author.[1]

Hentoff worried that if stories such as this were allowed to die, it could have ominous implications for the entire nation. So does former Secret Service agent Dan Bongino.

"The libertarian in me thinks this was a very dangerous incident for civil liberties," said Bongino, who served in the elite Presidential Protective Division, guarding presidents Bill Clinton, George W. Bush, and Barack Obama.[2]

"She was a law-abiding citizen, so it's unfortunate there aren't more people who are upset about this because Miriam could be anyone," Carey family attorney Eric Sanders lamented in an interview. "She was a sister and a daughter. She was a mother," he added. ". . . That's why this issue should be on everyone's mind. This could have been your sister, your daughter. Everyone makes mistakes, but she didn't have to die."[3]

And that is why the Miriam Carey story matters: anyone can make a wrong turn, but no one should be killed for it.

The federal government should not be allowed to unjustly kill someone in broad daylight without consequences.

That is why I wrote this book: because Miriam's killing shouldn't have happened, and because of the sense of justice of Joseph Farah, editor and WND's chief executive officer. He was so touched by her story, and so outraged by her killing, that he made it his cause and personal crusade. Farah has been dedicated to getting to the bottom of the Carey case and uncovering the truth since the day she was shot. WND published more than eighty stories on Miriam Carey from 2013 to 2015.

Farah explained why WND has pursued this story so persistently:

> The apparent state execution of Miriam Carey became my obsession. I didn't know her. But from the very first day,

something seemed obviously and dreadfully awry to me with the official explanations.

It was so repugnant to me that the thought of it literally kept me awake at night. I grew to despise the cover-up, the total lack of transparency, the way the Congress of the United States gave the police officers a standing ovation that very day—as if the cops had done something heroic.

I often ponder why we hear so much protest and see so much more news coverage of other police shootings that are much more justifiable, much more understandable under the circumstances, tragic, as any violent death is, but occupying that gray area in which the victim bears some responsibility.

There's no gray area in the case of the Miriam Carey death. It was akin to a police firing squad. And it wasn't just local police who were involved. It included the Secret Service, some of the most highly trained cops in the world. The investigation was overseen by the U.S. Justice Department and the attorney general of the United States one who had been so critical of local police shootings.

All of this, and much more that I cannot even put into words, has caused me to be that person who remains obsessed about this case even now. It has caused me to spread my obsession to others. It has made this my cause.

And I pray to God that my obsession . . . will ultimately lead to justice being served—not because it will bring Miriam Carey back from the dead, but so that it might prevent future Miriam Careys from being so abused and so mistreated.[4]

Why did cops chase her, and why did they pull their guns? Even former officers expressed amazement that her pursuers did not try to stop her with such nonlethal means as strip spikes to puncture her tires.

And when officers finally did corral Carey, why did they shoot to death a defenseless woman?

Why did they do anything to her?

Why didn't they just let her go?

Why didn't they just let her live?

# 1

# MEDIA VERSUS REALITY

IT WAS A PICTURE-POSTCARD perfect autumn day in the nation's capital on October 3, 2013: an inviting seventy-one degrees. Clear blue skies with just a wisp of clouds and hint of a breeze. A beautiful day for a drive.

No one knows if there was any other reason why Miriam Carey strapped her one-year-old daughter into the backseat of her black Nissan Infiniti and took the 265-mile journey from her home in Stamford, Connecticut, to Washington, D.C.

At 2:13 p.m., the young single mother apparently made a wrong turn into the White House guard post at Fifteenth and E Streets NW, because she immediately made a U-turn and attempted to leave.

Having failed to stop her from entering, Secret Service agents then tried to stop her from leaving.

Seven minutes later she would be dead.

What in the world went so wrong, so fast?

The media accounts of what happened turned out to be dead wrong. Here's what they reported on the day Carey was killed:

CBS said she "tried to ram the northeast gate of the White House" after "a heated exchange."[1] Carey did not ram a White House gate and she never exchanged words with anyone during the entire incident.

The Associated Press reported that she attempted to "penetrate the security barriers at both national landmarks [the White House and the Capitol]. . . . The pursuit began when the car sped onto a driveway leading to the White House."[2] Except it didn't. In fact, the statement from the uniformed Secret Service officer who tried to stop her said, she "was going slow."

The AP also reported that, according to a tourist, "When the driver couldn't get through a second barrier, she spun the car in the opposite direction, flipping a Secret Service officer over the hood of the car as she sped away."[3]

There was no second barrier, and she didn't "spin" her car in the opposite direction; she made a slow U-turn; and no one was flipped over her hood.

The *New York Times* also incorrectly reported that Carey was guilty of "ramming her way through barriers outside the White House and on Capitol Hill," adding, "Ms. Carey managed to get out of the car, and was shot by several officers."[4]

She never left her car. She was shot to death while sitting in her car.

"Ms. Carey sped down Pennsylvania Avenue toward the Capitol at speeds up to 80 miles per hour," the *Times* continued. Yet according to the *Washington Post*, she averaged 19.5 miles per hour.[5]

NBC joined the errant chorus, stating that Carey "tried to force her car through a White House security fence," further noting that a "Secret Service officer was struck by the woman's car."[6]

ABC reported that "a black Infiniti rammed a barrier outside the White House at 15th Street and Pennsylvania Avenue NW."[7] Only, the White House is about three blocks from that checkpoint and is not even visible from that intersection.

Echoing that Carey had struck "a security barrier and [a] U.S. Secret Service officer," CNN also reported that "when the woman drove up to a barrier at the 15th and E street checkpoint, she was approached by Secret Service officers who did not recognize her car."[8]

Officers did not approach her when she drove up to the post. As a matter of fact, they did not see her approach, and for some reason, didn't even notice her until she drove past them. Furthermore, there was no barrier facing her as she approached. A barrier was dragged in front of her car as she tried to leave.

"The motorist hurriedly tried to drive away, executed a three-point turn, struck the barrier and backed into an officer before driving away," a Secret Service source told CNN.[9]

But a witness said she drove away at average speed. She never backed into an officer.

After police discounted the notion that Carey posed a terrorist threat, the media next said she was on drugs. The toxicology report would later prove otherwise.

Then they portrayed her as mentally unbalanced, citing her struggle with postpartum depression.

She was killed because of baby blues? Something did not add up. Nothing added up.

After Carey departed the White House, she headed east on Pennsylvania Avenue. She ended up at Garfield Circle, where officers surrounded her car but failed to box her in with their vehicles.

As officers drew their guns, pointed them at her, and began shouting at the young mother, Carey fled.

Officers followed her up Constitution Avenue, where her path was blocked by a raised barricade at a U.S. Capitol Police guard post, about a block from the Capitol.

Carey turned her car around, but what exactly happened then is a matter of some dispute, as the witness accounts do not square with the official version of events.

The one thing that did happen indisputably was officers shot a woman in the back, who carried not even so much as a plastic fork with which to protect herself, and killed her as she sat in her car.

## WHERE'S THE OUTRAGE?

The killing of unarmed African-Americans has become a powder-keg issue in America. But not in the case of Miriam Carey.

There was a stark contrast between the reactions to the deadly shooting of this unarmed black woman and the wall-to-wall media coverage and outrage generated over the killing of unarmed black males Trayvon Martin and Michael Brown.

There were national protests and riots after the police shooting of the eighteen-year-old Brown in Ferguson, Missouri.

Not so for Carey.

Seventeen-year-old Martin was shot and killed during a struggle on February 26, 2012, in Sanford, Florida, with a Hispanic neighborhood watch coordinator. George Zimmerman claimed self-defense and was acquitted of murder.

President Obama ordered a federal investigation into Martin's death, saying, "It is absolutely imperative that we investigate every aspect of this. . . . If I had a son, he'd look like Trayvon . . . When I think about this boy, I think about my own kids."[10]

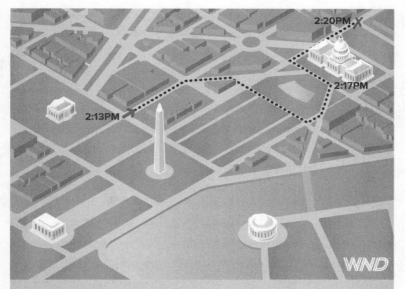

## MIRIAM CAREY'S ROUTE October 3, 2013

Left the Secret Service guard post at the White House at 2:13 p.m.

Drove southeast on Pennsylvania Ave.

Turned right at 3rd St. SW.

Made the first left at Maryland Ave. SW and
entered Garfield Circle at 2:17 p.m.

> She was shot at 8 times at Garfield Circle by
> 2 Secret Service officers and 1 Capitol Police officer.

Drove north on First St. NW and turned right onto Constitution.

Crashed at a Capitol Police guard post at 2nd St. NE and
Maryland Ave NE at 2:20 p.m.

> She was shot at 18 times at 2nd and Maryland,
> 9 by a Secret Service officer and 9 by a Capitol Police officer.

After Zimmerman was acquitted, the president added, "You know, when Trayvon Martin was first shot, I said that this could have been my son. Another way of saying that is Trayvon Martin could have been me 35 years ago."[11]

Rev. Al Sharpton said, "Trayvon could have been any one of our sons," and, "Trayvon could have been any one of us."[12]

Martin's death caused Rev. Jesse Jackson to claim that blacks were "under attack" because Obama's election had "triggered tremendous backlash."

"Targeting, arresting, convicting blacks and ultimately killing us is big business," insisted Jackson.[13]

The Justice Department investigation found there was not enough evidence for a federal hate crime prosecution of Zimmerman.

Eighteen-year-old Brown was shot and killed during a struggle on August 9, 2014, in Ferguson, Missouri, with a white police officer. A grand jury did not find enough evidence to indict officer Darren Wilson. The Justice Department conducted its own investigation and cleared Wilson of any civil rights violations. Additionally, the inquiry confirmed the officer's version of events: that he killed Brown in self-defense.

While ordering the federal investigation into Brown's death, Obama said in an official White House statement, "Michelle and I send our deepest condolences to his family and his community at this very difficult time."

The statement also said, "Aggressively pursuing investigations such as this is critical for preserving trust between law enforcement and the communities they serve."[14]

In his eulogy for Brown, Sharpton declared, "This is about justice! This is about fairness!"[15]

After the grand jury declined to indict Wilson, Sharpton

warned, "You won the first round, Mr. Prosecutor, but don't cut your gloves off, because the fight is not over. Justice will come to Ferguson!"[16]

Jackson topped them all in his indignation, calling the shooting of Brown "kind of a state execution."[17] He also said, "It seemed to me that the police act as judge, jury, and executioner."[18]

Where was the outrage for Carey?

Obama said nothing.

Sharpton said nothing.

Jackson said nothing.

When I requested comments from Jackson and Sharpton, their press representatives seemed impressed about the basic facts of the Carey case and requested more information.

Sharpton never responded.

Jackson's personal assistant, with whom I spoke with on the phone in November 2015, seemed particularly interested and said she would ask her boss about doing an interview with me.

A follow-up request in an e-mail a week later went unanswered. I sent another follow-up e-mail in February:

> One last followup note to see if Rev. Jackson would like to discuss the Miriam Carey case before my deadline.
>
> To refresh: She was an unarmed black woman who committed no crimes but was shot in the back and killed by the Secret Service and Capitol Police -- with her infant in the back of her car.
>
> My questions would be:
>
> • Were you aware of the Miriam Carey killing, and, if so, why have you been relatively silent on this shocking death?

- Did you or your organization offer to help the family?

- Do you think the Michael Brown case in Ferguson is somehow a worse example of police abuse than the Miriam Carey case, and, if so, how?

- Would your silence on the Carey case have anything to do with your support for the Obama administration?

Jackson's assistant responded positively, replying: "Thank you for your request. When is your deadline? Let's try to make it happen. Thank you so much."

But after that, crickets.

I can only suspect it was that last question I would have asked the reverend that stopped him in his tracks. Accusing the Ferguson cops of a virtual "state execution" was one thing. Accusing Obama's own police of the same thing may have seemed quite another.

In my pursuit of the truth, I contacted more than one hundred members of Congress, including every member of the Congressional Black Caucus, and informed them of the serious questions involved in the deadly shooting of Carey.

There was not one response.

Twice more I reached out to more than thirty lawmakers. There was one reply from a congressional aide who said that some members of the House Homeland Security Committee (which oversees the Secret Service) were interested and had asked for more information. But after providing it, I never heard from them, even after I had made additional inquiries.

It is not hard to imagine that members of Congress may have been reluctant to investigate the very police agency whose job it is to protect them.

In fact, the most notable congressional response to the killing of Carey was a thirty-five-second standing ovation, ostensibly in appreciation of Capitol Police for their protection.[19]

Members of Congress might be excused for not knowing the details of the Capitol Hill shooting on the same day it occurred. But in the days, weeks, months, and years to come, Congress would show remarkably little interest in discovering whether police had really protected lawmakers that fateful day—or had, instead, gunned down an innocent woman.

A few members of Congress finally showed at least a little interest in the Carey case on March 23, 2014, when they asked Capitol Police Chief Kim Dine a smattering of questions during a congressional hearing. Dine justified his officers' deadly response: "These officers are out there every day putting their lives on the line and they have to make split-second decisions, and it's easy for any one of us to obviously sit here and second guess them." After all, he told the House Appropriations Committee, which oversees his department, the car chase from the White House to the Capitol had involved a "very quick, very fluid set of circumstances."[20]

When Rep. James Moran (D-VA) asked Dine if officers should have shot at the tires rather than the driver—especially considering Carey was unarmed and had her baby in the backseat—the chief avoided answering the question, saying instead, "There's a lot of opinions out there, but most of them are wrong and uneducated."

"His comments are laughable," Carey family attorney Eric Sanders told me in an interview, as he disputed what he saw as the "shoot first, ask later" approach used by federal officers.

Sanders, a former New York police officer, said he was certain the officers who shot at Carey did not follow training guidelines. "If he's telling me that's the way law enforcement officers are trained in the District of Columbia, especially Capitol Police, then Congress and the rest of the district should be afraid, because that's not how you want your police officers responding." Sanders added, "What law enforcement tends to do is close ranks. If he's so confident in his statement, they could have released the [use of force] policy already. It's very easy."

Since the shooting, the officer-turned-attorney repeatedly tried to get the Justice Department (DOJ) to launch an investigation into the killing. Instead, the department eventually announced on July 10, 2014, that there was "insufficient evidence to pursue federal criminal civil rights or local charges against officers from the U.S. Secret Service and U.S. Capitol Police."[21]

But the department never explained why such overwhelming and deadly force was used against a weaponless woman and her child. To this day, the public barely knows who Carey was, as media coverage became practically nonexistent after her killing. It took more than a year for other media to catch up with my findings and do any significant follow-up on the Carey case. Even then, coverage was sparse.

The *Washington Post* published an excellent piece by David Montgomery on November 26, 2014, that highlighted many important questions and discrepancies in the official version of events. Montgomery noted how the twenty-six bullets fired at Carey set the case apart because shootings by Secret Service and Capitol Police officers are very rare. In fact, "White House guards didn't resort to their weapons in September, when fence-jumper Omar Gonzalez, who had a knife in his pocket, ran far into the executive mansion before being tackled. Carey was unarmed."[22]

Gonzalez was just one of seventeen White House fence jumpers since 1999. Not one of them was shot. Since 1912, there have been thirty-two attempted or successful breeches of White House security. Four of those intruders were shot; only one died. Those who were not shot include:

- Marshall H. Fields (1974) and Steven B. Williams (1976), each of whom was arrested after crashing a vehicle into a White House gate[23]

- Anthony Henry, who, armed with a knife, jumped the fence and cut two officers before being wrestled to the ground (1978)[24]

- Francisco Martin Duran, who fired twenty-nine rounds from a rifle at the White House from the sidewalk before passersby tackled him (1994)[25]

- Joseph Clifford Reel, who crashed a driverless jeep filled with hundreds of bullets, eight knives, and two machetes into a White House security gate as a diversion so he could spray paint a slogan on the side of the White House (2013)[26]

- Ricardo Burch, who jumped the fence and ran through the main floor of the White House with a knife before being tackled by a counterassault agent (2014)[27]

In contrast, suburban mom Miriam Carey, gunless and knifeless, simply made a wrong turn near the White House gate entrance and immediately tried to leave, never once doing anything to indicate she either wanted to enter White House grounds or do anyone any harm—and was shot.

But she wasn't just shot and killed. She was chased down and dispatched with devastating force. Yet, instead of reacting with outrage, black leaders have reacted with silence.

As has the rest of the world.

### WHO WAS MIRIAM?

Miriam Carey was a beautiful, successful, and vivacious young woman with a million-dollar smile. It's difficult to find a picture of her in which she was not beaming from ear to ear.

Miriam Carey at Niagara Falls in 2007. Photo courtesy Valarie Carey.

Carey was a thirty-four-year-old single mother, and her infant daughter, Erica, was the light of her life. She worked as a dental hygienist in Ardsley, New York, twenty-four miles from her home in Stamford, Connecticut.

"She always talked about teaching," Miriam's sister Amy told CNN. "She wanted to go further and give back in the field."[28]

Office manager Barbara Nicholson told the *Washington Post* that Carey was "one of the nicest people" she'd ever hired.[29]

"She was full of life, passionate about everything she did," another coworker told the paper.

"Miriam loved life and she loved her family," reflected sister Valarie Carey to WND's Michael Carl in a far-reaching and emotional interview in 2014. "She was a very loving and caring person. But she was also very goal-oriented and optimistic."[30]

Valarie said Miriam's daughter was the apple of her eye.

"She was good at bringing together friends and family. She was good at making people laugh. She was good at debating different topics and really good at keeping family relationships active and positive. She was a bridge to bring people together. My sister was not a criminal. My sister was a law-abiding citizen and she didn't commit any crimes while she was in the District of Columbia," insisted Valarie, who is a former New York City Police Department sergeant. "It's one of the reasons why this whole thing makes no sense at all. This has just shattered our lives. It shattered our family. It was so unexpected, so unjust, so unfair, so untimely."

Sanders, who met Miriam a few years before her death, recalled that she was enthusiastic and upbeat, telling Carl, "She was someone you would trust with your life. I think what happened is that first she was portrayed as a woman with a gun. That was inaccurate. Then it was a crazy person driving around. Of course, we don't value crazy people in this world. So we can discard them. She didn't mean anything, and that's how it's been portrayed so far."

Indeed, after it became apparent Carey was neither armed nor a terrorist, the media immediately theorized that she was crazy.

Just one day after the shooting, ABC News reported that their "sources revealed that Carey had started to show signs of mental illness around September 2012, and had a history of delusions and irrational behavior."[31]

Who were those anonymous sources?

The police.

"Carey had an encounter with Stamford police in December 2012 that resulted in her being taken for a mental health evaluation, law enforcement sources told CBS News's Bob Orr," reported the network the day after the shooting.[32]

And police were the only source of these stories.

A Stamford, Connecticut, police report filed on November 11, 2012, recorded that Carey had told officers that "Stamford and the state of Connecticut [were] on a security lock down. She stated that President Obama put Stamford in lockdown after speaking to her because she is the Prophet of Stamford. She further stated that President Obama had put her residence under electronic surveillance and that it was being fed live to all the national news outlets."[33]

But the problem with the theory that she was crazy is that those who knew her best reported no incidents or signs of "delusions and irrational behavior." That is, no one except the man who had called police, the estranged father of Carey's child, Eric Francis.

And he has refused to speak with media unless he is paid.

Francis apparently called Stamford police to deal with Carey a number of times, but the last incident was more than nine months before her fatal trip to Washington.

"And for him to call the police because she's in the bathroom and the baby is crying, that was uncalled for. You're not capable of soothing a baby, and you have to call the police?" Valarie told the *Post*.

Francis even called police when he simply couldn't find Carey.

"One of those calls," Valarie told the paper, "came from the night that my sister was here [in Brooklyn], and she left here late, and then she went home, and he's calling the police? . . . He didn't call my mother. He didn't call us."[34]

Four days after the shooting, sisters Amy and Valarie confirmed on CNN that Miriam had been diagnosed with an extremely rare condition called postpartum psychosis, a few months after her daughter had been born.[35] The disorder can cause delusions and paranoia, but her sisters said there was no evidence of that in Miriam's case.

"There were not moments of her walking around with delusions. That was not what was going on," Amy told CNN.[36]

"She was not walking around delusional," affirmed Valarie on NBC's *Today* show, adding, "My sister was not a bipolar schizophrenic individual."[37]

"There wasn't a pattern. It was something that occurred suddenly. She seemed overwhelmed," said Amy on CNN. "There was a lot of stress."[38]

Amy told the *Today* show's Matt Lauer, "She worked very closely with her doctor to taper her off the medication. It wasn't something that was displayed. It was a momentary breakdown . . . She didn't appear to be unstable."

Miriam's mother, Idella Carey, also told reporters her daughter was hospitalized after a "momentary breakdown" in the months after giving birth. But according to the family, Carey soon turned her life around and, by all accounts, was perfectly fine and happy during the months that followed.

Coworker Nicholson told the *Washington Post* that Carey was "absolutely normal." She went on to say, "There was no indication she ever had issues. You couldn't ask for a more professional person than her. No one ever complained about her, and that's highly unusual. She was the sweetest person you ever want to know."[39]

Amy, Valarie, and Miriam Carey at Niagara Falls in 2007. Photo courtesy Valarie Carey.

Sanders argued that Carey's mental state was entirely irrelevant to the shooting, and that, whatever it was, it was not a reason to kill her. "I don't care if she suffered from 15 mental conditions!" the attorney told me as far back as late 2013. "And, by the way, police are trained to deal with those types of situations, too. So you can disregard that. We don't know [her mental condition]. The only thing we know is that the police pulled the trigger.

"Police were not justified in discharging their weapons. So, for us it [her mental state] is a non-issue."[40]

"The media tried to depict my sister as some kind of mentally ill person," woefully reflected Valarie. "For some reason, that makes people think it was sort of okay that she was shot. She was not mentally ill. She had postpartum depression. If that's a reason to kill a person, that's a very sad lesson."

"I don't know why Miriam went to D.C. that day," Valarie told the *Washington Post*. "But what I do know is that she was killed in D.C. that day . . . The emphasis shouldn't be on why was she there. The emphasis should be what those officers did. Were their actions proper?"[41]

Writing in *National Review* one month after the shooting, columnist Mark Steyn observed:

Ms. Carey does not appear to be guilty of any act other than a panic attack when the heavy-handed and heavier-armed palace guard began yelling at her. Much of what was reported in the hours after her death seems dubious: We are told Ms. Carey was "mentally ill," although she had no medications in her vehicle and those at her home back in Connecticut are sufficiently routine as to put millions of other Americans in the category of legitimate target. We are assured that she suffered from post-partum depression, as if the inability to distinguish between a depressed mom and a suicide bomber testifies to the officers' professionalism. Under D.C. police rules, cops are not permitted to fire on a moving vehicle, because of the risk to pedestrians and other drivers. But the Secret Service and the Capitol Police enjoy no such restraints, so the car doors are full of bullet holes.[42]

The impression that Carey had been dispatched in a manner akin to a state execution spawned wild Internet rumors that she had given birth to Obama's love child and was killed to keep the affair secret. The Carey family has strongly denied those rumors, or having anything to do with them.

The leading proponent of the conspiracy theory, Rev. James David Manning, told the *National Enquirer*, "Why else would police take such drastic measures to stop Miriam Carey—an innocent person?" adding, "Her tragic death smacks of a cover-up."[43]

Carey family attorney and former NYPD officer Eric Sanders.

Sanders agrees there was a cover-up, but not to protect Obama. He ridiculed a claim by Manning that Valarie had asked Obama to take a paternity test.[44]

When I asked Sanders about it, the attorney said, "I've asked for a retraction, and so far they haven't gotten back to me. I'm pretty annoyed about that,"

Sanders said. "That's not what we said. We are not game-players. We're serious people. We don't do those kinds of things." He told me his experience as a police officer had led him to understand that sometimes even those dedicated to serve and to protect do things that are hard to understand, or even believe. "The bottom line is, cops do a lot of outrageous things. They really do. The public really has no clue as to what is really going on. You really have to be from that [police] culture to really understand what they are doing."

And that's why, he said, you can't believe everything you see in the news.

"Quite frankly, they are underreporting a lot of things. It's not as isolated as people think it is; it's a really big problem. It's just that cops won't speak up about it. Let me tell you, the blue wall of silence is serious—hurting other cops and other outrageous things—that really does happen."[45]

# 2

# POLICE VERSUS REALITY

AFTER THE EVIDENCE SURROUNDING the shooting death of Miriam Carey was finally unearthed, it did not match the official version of events at all.

After much digging it was eventually discovered:

- Miriam Carey was shot in the back

- Officers claimed they shot her in self-defense

- Her child was covered in glass and blood and hospitalized

- Carey didn't break any laws

- Carey didn't try to enter the White House grounds

- Carey did not ram a White House gate

- Officers gave no reason for stopping Carey

- Officers gave no reason for pursuing Carey

- Carey did not flee or speed away

- Carey did not run over an officer

- Police likely knew Carey was not a terrorist before they shot her

- Secret Service officers violated their own use of force policy

- Capitol Police violated their own use of force policy

- Secret Service officers violated their own vehicular pursuit policy

- Capitol Police officers violated their own vehicular pursuit policy

- Police statements were missing

- Witness statements were missing

- Evidence was missing

- Police refused to release findings justifying the shooting

This is the series of steps made to obtain the evidence used to make those revelations:

- Filing a FOIA request for surveillance video and the forensics report

- Visiting the shooting scene and discovering at least seven surveillance cameras

- Speaking to an officer who confirmed the existence of video of the Carey shooting

- Obtaining a copy of the unpublished Secret Service policies on vehicle pursuits

- Obtaining a copy of the unpublished Capitol Police policies on the use of force and vehicle pursuits

- Making a FOIA request to MPD for the police report and all evidence

- After that was denied, successfully appealing the FOIA request to the office of the Washington, D.C., mayor

- Discovering the police report was missing key evidence

- Making a FOIA request for all evidence and police reports to the Justice Department

- After the Justice Department stonewalled, enlisting Judicial Watch to sue the government to compel compliance

- Taking the Justice Department back to court after the response to the FOIA request was incomplete

It is one of the eccentricities of Washington's legal system that the Secret Service is subject to FOIA requests but the U.S. Capitol Police Department is not.

As previously noted, even after the Justice Department complied and turned over additional information, much key evidence was still missing.

As this book was being published, Judicial Watch was pressing the Justice Department in federal court for the missing material, a process that could take another half year to play out.

It should be noted that the enlistment of Judicial Watch provided a significant boost to the quest for justice for Carey. Judicial Watch has become a big-time power player in Washington, often obtaining materials from the Obama administration that even Congress has been unable to secure. It is because of the efforts of this nonpartisan foundation that a series of incriminating e-mails from Lois Lerner became public. Lerner is the central figure in the IRS scandal, as the former head of the tax-exempt division who illegally targeted conservative groups for scrutiny.

Judicial Watch has also uncovered critical information on the terrorist attack that killed U.S. ambassador Chris Stevens and three other Americans in Benghazi, Libya; Obama's executive orders granting immigration amnesty; the Fast and Furious gunrunning scheme; the swap of five top Taliban leaders for Sgt. Bowe Bergdahl (later charged with desertion); and the official e-mails former secretary of state Hillary Clinton kept on a private server, many of which they have obtained.

Although often characterized by the media as a conservative watchdog group, Judicial Watch has not played favorites, suing former vice president Dick Cheney and several members of Halliburton's board of directors in 2002 over accounting practices.

After filing suit on behalf of WND, Judicial Watch president Tom Fitton said, "The illegal secrecy by the Justice Department has forced our journalist client, WND, to go to federal court to get its simple questions answered." He further said, "Given the Obama Justice Department's habit of second-guessing police officers in shooting incidents, it is the height of hypocrisy for Eric Holder's DOJ to violate FOIA law to keep secret details about the controversial shooting of Miriam Carey, who also happens to be black, by federal law enforcement."[1]

In this chapter, we will compare the facts to the fiction, fleshing out the details in the evidence.

## 1. CAREY DID NOT TRY TO ENTER THE WHITE HOUSE

As stated earlier, Miriam Carey never tried to enter the White House. She never even tried to enter the grounds. The first and only thing she did after turning in to a White House guard post was make a U-turn and try to leave, which is not illegal. She never threatened anyone.

It is the job of the uniformed Secret Service officers at White House guard posts to prevent unauthorized people from trying to enter. It is not their job to prevent people from trying to leave, but that is precisely what happened.

The problem, then, didn't begin because Carey turned in at the guard post. The problem began because, judging from the available evidence, no one was manning the post.

In fact, there is no evidence that any of the officers on duty saw her drive up to the entrance or were even there to greet her, check her identification, or stop her from proceeding. Furthermore, the statement by the Secret Service agent on duty does not say he saw her car approach or that he tried to stop

Photo provided by U.S. Attorney.

her at the entrance. This indicates that he was either not at the post, or was not manning it properly and failed to see her until she had driven past him.

According to what the police report described as "a brief synopsis" of the guard's witness interview:

> Officer [redacted] states that he was at his assigned post along with Officer [redacted] the guard shack at 15th and E St NW when a black car came onto the White House grounds. The driver did not stop at the guard shack as required by protocol so I could check her ID. She just kept going. I hit on the back end of the car to try to get it to stop, and she still didn't stop. She wasn't going fast. As she got [to] the next set of barracks she made a U-turn and came back towards us. At this time she came to a stop or slowed down to an almost stop, I tried to open the front driver's door but it was locked. I noticed that there was a baby in the car. Officer attempted to stop the vehicle by putting bike rack in its path. The car stopped then accelerated and officer was knocked off his feet and over the vehicle. A look was broadcast as the vehicle traveled west on Pennsylvania Ave. The driver was a black female wearing a pink hat. She did not make any eye contact with me. I hit the car several times to get her to stop and she just kept stirring [sic] straight ahead.

So, based on this report, the officer apparently didn't see Carey's car at all until she was preparing to make a U-turn to immediately try to leave. The report also indicates that Carey made no attempt to breach security; neither did she pose any threat because, not only was she trying to leave, she "wasn't going fast."

The security video shot at the guard post would show

exactly what happened, but authorities, without explanation, have refused to release it, and it was not provided even though the FOIA request was for all materials used in the investigation.

In fact, the guard's actual statement was not even released. The video and the statement are just two of numerous pieces of evidence authorities failed to provide in response to the FOIA request.

An incident similar to Carey's, just a half a year after her fateful turn at the White House, lends credence to the possibility that security at the guard posts was lax.

On May 6, 2014, a man driving a gray Honda Civic turned in to a White House checkpoint at Seventeenth Street and Pennsylvania Avenue, right behind a motorcade carrying President Obama's two daughters.

The Secret Service took fifty-five-year-old Mathew Evan Goldstein into custody, causing the White House to go into lockdown for an hour. According to his schedule, President Obama was inside the building at the time, meeting with Secretary of State John Kerry.

It turned out, Goldstein was an IRS employee who had a pass for the U.S. Treasury building, located right next to the White House on Pennsylvania Avenue. It appears that, just like Carey, he simply made a wrong turn into a security gate and suddenly found himself the target of law enforcement.

Unlike Carey, he did not pay for his mistake with his life.

According to Carey family attorney Sanders, the fact that the driver was able to enter the secure area so easily proved what he had been saying all along about federal law enforcement agents and Carey: "Their negligence caused her death," he told me. "Their security is terrible!"

## 2. CAREY DID NOT RAM A WHITE HOUSE GATE

Carey did not try to ram her way into the White House.

She did not try to ram her way onto the White House grounds.

She did not ram a White House fence, gate, or security barrier. Yet mainstream media outlets such as the *New York Times*, CNN, CBS, NBC, and ABC News all reported sensational accounts that Carey had done just that.

> NBC: "A woman who tried to force her car through a White House security fence Thursday afternoon was shot and killed by police after a 12-block chase past the Capitol, which was locked down for a half-hour, authorities said."[2]

> ABC: "A woman believed to be a dental hygienist from Stamford, Conn., was shot dead by police today after allegedly attempting to ram the White House gates and leading authorities on a high-speed chase to the U.S. Capitol, officials said."[3]

> CBS: "A Connecticut woman driving a black Infiniti with her 1-year-old daughter in the car tried to ram through a barricade Thursday, then led police on a chase that ended with her being shot to death, officials said."[4]

> CNN: "The motorist's black Infiniti, according to authorities, itself became a weapon Thursday afternoon, first striking a security barrier and U.S. Secret Service officer near the White House before hurtling down some of the capital's most famous streets, police cruisers in pursuit."[5]

> *NY Daily News*: "There was horror on the Hill when a crazed Connecticut woman who tried to ram her way into the White

House was shot and killed Thursday after leading police on a high-speed chase through the heart of Washington."[6]

*New York Times*: "A woman with a young child was shot to death after turning her vehicle into a weapon on Thursday afternoon, ramming her way through barriers outside the White House and on Capitol Hill."[7]

And where did the media get the idea that Carey had tried to "ram her way through" a security fence, gate, or barrier?

From "officials."

Fox: "Officials said the incident began with a car chase, which started when the suspect, driving a black sedan with Connecticut plates, tried to ram a barrier near the White House."[8]

Washington's top cop, Police Chief Cathy Lanier, even "dismissed any suggestion that she had tried to breach security by accident and said the officers 'acted heroically.'"[9]

However, the accounts given in the media differ markedly from what witnesses stated in the police report.

Not one witness, either a civilian or an officer, said Carey hit a White House fence. Or a security barrier.

She hit a bike rack.

A large man in plain clothes, who turned out to be an off-duty Secret Service officer, dragged the bike rack in front of Carey's car at the end of the driveway to the guard post, as she was trying to leave.

Far from targeting the bike rack, she tried to drive around it.

But the off-duty officer dragged it right back in front of her car.

The only "barrier" Carey's car hit wasn't protecting the White House. It wasn't protecting anything.

This is how the police report described what a witness told investigators:

> A male was pulling a gate in front of the vehicle to keep the vehicle in the area. The vehicle attempted to flee the area but the man pulled the gate back in front of the vehicle. The vehicle then hit the gate knocking this man to the ground.

The Secret Service officer who tried to stop Carey at the White House guard post told police, "Officer attempted to stop the vehicle by putting [a] bike rack in its path."

That bike rack is the only mention in the police report of any "fence," "barrier," or "gate" at the White House.

The "Event Chronology" by the Internal Affairs Division of the MPD stated, "Officer [redacted] of the USSS was off-duty and walking by the checkpoint when he observed Officers [redacted] and [redacted] attempting to stop Ms. Carey. In an effort to assist, Officer [redacted] placed a bicycle rack in the path of Ms. Carey's vehicle, but she failed to stop."

As the photo on the previous page shows, the off-duty officer leaned on the bike rack to try to prevent Carey from leaving.

You can also see that the officer was in civilian clothes and was carrying a cooler. This photo was one of only a few released by the U.S. Attorney to the public, and the cooler is plainly visible. There is no evidence that the man who carried it ever identified himself as a law enforcement officer as he tried to stop Carey.

Sanders said it was not unreasonable to ask if the officer was intoxicated, given that he was carrying that cooler.

### 3. CAREY DID NOT RUN OVER OR ASSAULT AN OFFICER
I have also confirmed that Carey neither hit nor ran over an officer, again contrary to what the media reported.

> NBC: "As she fled east on Pennsylvania Ave., she struck a Secret Service officer, and a chase ensued."[10]

> ABC: "In fleeing the White House scene, the suspect hit a Secret Service officer with her car."[11]

> CNN: "The motorist's black Infiniti . . . [struck] a . . . U.S. Secret Service officer near the White House."[12]

> FOX: "Rep. Michael McCaul, R-Texas, chairman of the House Homeland Security Committee, told Fox News that the woman originally tried to run down a Secret Service agent near the White House. The Secret Service later confirmed the officer was struck by the woman's car."[13]

Again, here's what a witness told police: "A male was pulling a gate in front of the vehicle to keep the vehicle in the area. The vehicle attempted to flee the area but the man pulled the gate back in front of the vehicle. The vehicle then hit the gate knocking this man to the ground."

That witness indicated that Carey tried to drive around the off-duty officer, "but the man pulled the gate back in front of the vehicle."

Another witness told police: "A large framed male with a cooler pulled a barrier to block this vehicle. The black vehicle hit the barrier which knocked the man to the ground."

Photo provided by U.S. Attorney.

Even the police's own description of Carey's encounter with the off-duty officer confirms she did not hit him; she hit the gate, which "spun around" and hit him.

On the document titled "Metropolitan Police Department Incident Summary Sheet," the synopsis read: "The United States Secret Service police officer attempted to block the vehicle with a bicycle rack; however, the vehicle pushed over the bicycle rack, which spun around knocking the officer over."

Additionally, the police affidavit requesting a search warrant stated Carey's "vehicle pushed over the bicycle rack, knocking the officer to the ground."

Finally, the *New York Times* published this account from a tourist who was standing near the White House: "One of the guys grabbed one of those little metal fence sections and shoved it in front of her, across the driveway. She hit the brakes slightly and tried to get around it on the right, but the guy shoved it in front of her again, to try to keep her in."[14]

Precisely what happened could have been verified if the Justice Department had provided video of the encounter at the guard post, but the department, without explanation, failed to include that key bit of evidence in response to the FOIA request.

## 4. OFFICERS GAVE NO REASON FOR STOPPING CAREY

Oddly enough, the police report does not explain why Secret Service officers tried to stop Carey from leaving the scene. No government official has ever explained it either. And since she had not violated any laws, it is especially puzzling that officers did, in fact, try to stop her. Why would they?

They never said.

What one Secret Service officer at the post did say was, "The driver did not stop at the guard shack as required by protocol so I could check her ID. She just kept going."

But she did not need an ID to leave. She would have needed one only to enter. So the question is, how did she manage to drive right by officers in the first place?

"You know how she got past them? Because they were over there, smoking and joking and lackadaisical, just like I said from the beginning," attorney Sanders told me, unapologetically. "That's why they don't want to show the video."

Put simply, the guard was not at his post.

## 5. CAREY DID NOT BREAK ANY LAWS

During my discussion with Sanders he noted that the application for the search warrant for Carey's car never accused her of violating any laws—at all.

To obtain a search warrant, he explained, officers were required to show probable cause that a crime had been committed. But the warrant application itself shows nothing of the kind, no proof of a criminal act whatsoever. Instead, the affidavit filed by the Washington, D.C., Metropolitan Police Department in support of the search warrant merely accused Carey of violating "several traffic regulations."

Under the heading "Subject of Force," the police report did state: "Violations during police contact: Assault on a Police Officer (APO) DC Code 22 Sec 404." The thing is, Section 22-404 of the criminal code of the District of Columbia isn't "Assault on a Police Officer."

It's general assault.

Section 22-405 is assault on a police officer.

Under Title 22, Chapter 4 of the D.C. criminal code:

§ 22-404 is: "Assault or threatened assault in a menacing manner; stalking."

§ 22-405 is: "Assault on member of police force, campus or university special police, or fire department."

Sanders, the former NYPD officer-turned-attorney, told me police did not cite the specific code referencing an assault on a police officer because they knew that would never stand up under scrutiny or in court.

Another reason police did not cite the code on assaulting an officer may have been because the Secret Service officer who confronted Carey was off duty. And remember: the police report does not indicate that this officer, who was in plainclothes, ever identified himself as a law enforcement officer.

Not one witness said he did.

His fellow officers did not say he did.

So what Carey saw was a large man in a T-shirt and shorts, carrying a cooler and dragging a bike rack in front of her car as she lawfully tried to exit the guard post and drive onto Pennsylvania Ave.

The off-duty officer undoubtedly gave a statement to investigators. But for whatever reason, no such statement was included in the FOIA material. So the only indication that exists that the plainclothesman was an "officer" is in the statement prepared by the officer on duty at the guard post, after the fact:

"Officer attempted to stop the vehicle by putting bike rack in its path."

Carey had no way of knowing the man in front of her car was an officer.

And, given that he had not identified himself, Sanders told me, she would not be legally culpable for assaulting an officer, even if she had assaulted him.

## 6. CAREY DID NOT FLEE OR SPEED AWAY

For someone accused of trying to "flee" from officers, isn't it peculiar that the first thing Carey did after exiting the White House guard post was stop at a red light? That's precisely what one witness said she did: "Mr. [redacted] states that marked police vehicles with lights and sirens began chasing the vehicle. It is the belief of this witness that the vehicle stopped at a traffic light," the police report reads.

In fact, not only did Carey apparently first stop at a traffic light, but the evidence indicates that she then proceeded to drive in the direction of the Capitol "at an average speed," according to another witness. A third witness stated that "the speed of vehicles was approximately forty miles per hour when the vehicles passed her." That's a far cry from the speeds of up to eighty miles per hour that the Justice Department statement claimed.

Actually, she may have been traveling significantly slower in her drive down Pennsylvania Avenue from the White House to the Capitol. The *Washington Post* calculated Carey's average speed along that route at "19.5 mph in a 25-mph zone," given the distance traveled and the time it took her to get there.[15]

And her average speed from the Capitol to the spot where the chase ended on Constitution at Second and Maryland was "42 mph."

In response to our FOIA request, the Justice Department turned over video showing traffic on Pennsylvania Avenue between the White House and the Capitol during the time frame in which Carey drove that route.

The video shows no sign of a high-speed chase.[16]

## 7. BAD INFORMATION MAY HAVE LED TO POLICE CHASE

A statement from a Secret Service officer explained that he joined the chase of Carey after hearing a radio call to be on the lookout for a black Infiniti "that had just rammed barriers that protected the White House."

What was the source of that bad information?

It appears to have come from either the Secret Service guard who reported the incident to headquarters and/or the dispatcher who sent out the radio call to police.

The Secret Service officer was asked to explain in a witness statement "how . . . he became involved in the incident near the White House." The police report summary of his statement reads, "Officer explained that he was on patrol near White House when he heard an officer from one of the fixed posts go over the radio zone that he had a priority." It further explains that "Officer responded to location where he received a lookout [a report to "be on the lookout"] for a black Infinity [*sic*] with Connecticut [plates] that had just rammed barriers that protected the White House."

The officer said he then jumped into the passenger seat of a marked Secret Service vehicle and ended up at Garfield Circle.

The officer's statement might explain why he and other officers pursued Carey with such ferocity and eventually used deadly force to stop her. They could easily have believed they were trying to stop someone who had tried to commit an act of terrorism, having been told she "had just rammed barriers that protected the White House."

Except, it wasn't true.

As we now know, she had actually hit a bike rack.

But somewhere, the truth appears to have gotten lost in translation, and that may have cost Carey her life.

## 8. POLICE KNEW OF THE CHILD IN CAREY'S CAR

According to the police report, the Secret Service officer who first encountered Carey at the White House guard post told investigators that after she entered the post, made a U-turn, and came back toward the exit, "she came to a stop or slowed down to an almost stop, I tried to open the front driver's door but it was locked. I noticed that there was a baby in the car."

That was Carey's baby girl, strapped into a child car seat in the backseat, on the right side of the vehicle.

Since that first officer knew there was a child in the car, doesn't it stand to reason that all of the other law enforcement officers should also have known that immediately, the moment the radio report was broadcast?

Yes, they should have known that they were shooting at a car with an *infant* strapped into the backseat.

Yet, in its statement issued on July 10, 2014, the Justice Department said that the officers at the scene of the deadly shooting "*discovered* that there was a young child in the vehicle" (emphasis added) and that no charges would be filed against officers.[17]

Why the pursuing officers did not seem to know Carey's child was in the car was not explained in the police report.

Radio transmissions by police during the pursuit of Carey were not included in the FOIA material provided by the MPD or DOJ. "You know why?" Sanders asked rhetorically. "Because such information doesn't support their legal position."

According to an eyewitness interviewed by investigators, once Carey departed the White House guard post, agents got on their radios.

Did none of those who radioed in the report mention the child? Or did the dispatcher fail to inform the pursuing officers when the lookout was issued?

Worse yet, what if the information *was* radioed to officers—but they shot at Carey's car anyway?

"Thus far, it's unconfirmed if that information was ever broadcasted," Sanders told me. "However, according to a former uniformed Secret Service officer who contacted me, that information was transmitted over the air to the dispatcher who, in turn, notified the U.S. Capitol Police." The former officer was on duty and in the officers' locker room at the time he heard that radio call, he told Sanders, adding that he heard a number of other radio reports, until the chase ended with the deadly shooting of Carey.

Some have wondered if officers did not hear about the child before they shot because of communication lapses between the Secret Service and Capitol Police, and because of the Reagan-era radio system still in use by police at the time of the Carey chase. In fact, in March 2014, *Roll Call* reported that Rep. Debbie Wasserman Schultz (D-FL) grilled Capitol Police chief Kim Dine as to whether the antiquated radio system had hindered the department's response to the Carey incident.[18]

Wasserman Schultz said some police officers had told her the radios used during the chase and shooting were not capable of communicating with Secret Service officers.

According to Dine, two emergency channels and a mutual aid radio system allowed the two agencies to communicate. If that were true, would not officers have known of the child in the car?

And if they did know, why did they shoot?

"In any event, the officers' conduct was willful and absolutely reckless, a total disregard of Miriam's and her daughter's civil rights," Sanders maintained.

Reckless indeed. The rear of Carey's car, where the toddler was strapped in, was riddled with bullets. The rear window was shattered.

### 9. OFFICERS VIOLATED THEIR OWN POLICIES

According to government documents, federal officers violated their own rules on vehicle pursuits and the use of deadly force when they chased, shot, and killed Carey.

The Secret Service and Capitol Police do not make public their policies on firing upon moving vehicles. But Sanders obtained the secret and unpublished policy on vehicular pursuits from the U.S. Secret Service *Uniformed Division Operational Procedures* manual. The guidelines on the use of deadly force in the *Homeland Security Legal Division Handbook* are available to the public.[19]

Since 2003, the Secret Service has been part of the Department of Homeland Security, or DHS.

Sanders said the portions of the Secret Service manual relevant to the Carey case were provided by a former Secret Service officer who was on duty at the time of the chase and the deadly shooting.

"These documents are the smoking gun that prove federal officers wrongly killed Miriam Carey," claimed Sanders. "The discovery of these secret policies also proves the Department of Justice intentionally erred in declining to file criminal charges against the officers who pursued and killed Miriam Carey."

Sanders called it a cover-up by the Justice Department, saying, "They knew exactly what they were doing" by not pressing charges, even though officers "clearly violated their own policies."

The U.S. Secret Service Operational Procedures guidelines on "Vehicular Pursuits" states under the heading "General Policy":

> A member shall not become engaged in a vehicular pursuit except to effect the arrest or prevent the escape, when every other means of effecting the arrest or preventing the escape has been exhausted, of a person who has committed a felony or attempted to commit a felony in the member's presence, or when a felony has been committed and the member has reasonable grounds to believe the person he/she is attempting to apprehend has committed the felony; provided that the felony for which the arrest is sought involved an actual or threatened attack which the member has reasonable cause to believe could result in death or serious bodily injury.

Key here is the order prohibiting uniformed Secret Service members from becoming "engaged in a vehicular pursuit except to effect the arrest or prevent the escape" of a "person who has committed a felony or attempted to commit a felony." Recall that, not only did Carey not commit a felony, but officials never accused her of committing any crime whatsoever. Furthermore, nothing in the July 10, 2014, Justice Department statement exonerating officers said she committed any crimes to instigate the chase.

"There is nothing in the vehicle-pursuit policy that authorized the officers to pursue Miriam and her minor child," said Sanders.

Under that same heading in the U.S. Secret Service Operational Procedures guidelines on "Vehicular Pursuits," the text states:

> Whenever it becomes evident that injury to citizens or members of the Force, or unnecessary property damage may result

from a vehicular pursuit, that pursuit shall be immediately discontinued. *Safety is the first priority, not arrest.*

That last sentence is printed in bold in the manual. However, "safety" did not appear to be the "first priority" of the federal officers who pursued Carey.

Mangled wreck of a police cruiser that slammed into a pop-up security barrier while chasing Carey. Photo provided by Justice Department.

First they shot at Carey's moving car in Garfield Circle, surrounded by about thirty bystanders in the immediate vicinity, according to the police report. Scores, perhaps hundreds, of office workers, tourists, pedestrians, drivers, and even members of Congress may have been in the line of fire, given the close proximity of numerous government office buildings and busy streets.

Under "Pursuit Procedures," the manual states:

Members shall immediately discontinue the pursuit and notify the Control Center whenever conditions exist (e.g., weather conditions, roadway or pavement conditions, rush hour considerations, vehicular or pedestrian traffic congestion, speed of the pursuit, handling of the police vehicle) or become such that further vehicular pursuit would lead a reasonable person to believe that unnecessary property damage, or injury to citizens or members of the Force may result.

Police have never explained why it was so important to stop Carey that they felt at liberty to utterly disregard this policy.

The chase was so intense that a police cruiser accidentally slammed into a pop-up security barrier on Constitution Avenue with such force that witnesses thought they'd heard an explosion. The collision caused an injury to an officer requiring an airlift to the hospital. The officer recovered, but the chase was not immediately halted, even after that near tragedy.

"The officers and other employees assigned to the United States Secret Service Uniform Division clearly violated their own policies, especially the vehicle-pursuit policy, which clearly restricts its employees' ability to engage in high-risk vehicle pursuits favoring safety over apprehension," observed Sanders.

Also under "Pursuit Procedures," the manual states:

The pursuing vehicles shall be operated in accordance with the provisions set forth in this policy under "Operation of Emergency Vehicles," in particular that no pursuing vehicle shall be operated at a speed greater than ten miles per hour in excess of the posted or established speed limit.

If Carey really did speed toward the Capitol "at speeds up to 80 miles per hour," as the Justice Department claimed and the *New York Times* reported, then why did officers not suspend the pursuit, as this regulation requires?[20]

Under "Initiation of Pursuits," another guideline states:

> Vehicular pursuits, as authorized above, may be initiated by members operating authorized department vehicles after they have attempted, by using appropriate warning devices from a close proximity, to stop a violator who is already in a vehicle if the violator has (1) indicated by his/her actions that he/she is aware of the stop attempt, and (2) disregarded the stop attempt and attempted to flee in the vehicle.

As noted previously, Carey did not attempt to flee, according to the police report witness who said the first thing Carey did upon leaving the White House guard post was stop at a red light.

A witness also said Carey departed the White House at an average speed.

The Department of Homeland Security sets the Secret Service's guideline on when it is permissible for officers to use force. The pertinent section of the DHS *Legal Division Handbook* is titled, "There is No 'Perfect Answer' when Using Force." Under the heading, "Factors to Consider in Determining Whether Excessive Force was Used," the very first criterion listed is "Severity of the Crime." Remember that Carey had committed no crime.

"There is nothing in the vaguely written 'Use of Force' policy that authorized police personnel to discharge their service weapons toward Miriam and her minor child, resulting in Miriam's death," Sanders told me.

"Certainly," he added, "since the officers had no authority to pursue them, they cannot establish authority to use deadly physical force against Miriam or her minor child."

Officials have never even attempted to explain what crime Carey may have committed that would justify officers shooting and killing her.

Yet the Department of Justice found no reason to bring criminal charges against any officers.

Under the heading "Use of Deadly Force—Objective Reasonableness," the handbook states: "Where the officer has probable cause to believe that the suspect poses a threat of serious physical harm, either to the officer or to others, it is not constitutionally unreasonable to prevent escape by using deadly force."

A "threat"? Really? From what weapon? Carey didn't have one.

What about the argument that Carey was using her car as a deadly weapon? That was the impression the *New York Times* gave when it reported that she was shot "after turning her vehicle into a weapon" and "ramming her way through barriers."[21]

Sanders disagreed.

"She had a car. A car is not a deadly weapon. I don't care what these people keep saying, I've been in law enforcement a long time, training with all these different agencies. We all know law enforcement training is cars are not weapons."

Even the Metropolitan Police, which conducted the official investigation into the incident, agreed with Sanders, as MPD rules state, "[A] moving vehicle is not considered deadly force."[22]

Sanders, himself a former NYPD officer, said the entire deadly tragedy would have been avoided if pursuing officers had "attempted the 'PIT maneuver' meaning an attempted controlled intentional pushing of Miriam Carey's vehicle."

The PIT maneuver, or precision immobilization technique, is a pursuit tactic in which an officer uses his car to bump the side of another car from the rear, causing it to spin out and come to a stop. That or many other nonlethal tactics, such as the laying of spike strips, could have been used to stop Carey, Sanders told me.

Before publishing their policies and procedures on vehicle pursuit, WND wanted to ensure that doing so would not harm the ability of Secret Service officers to do their jobs. Legal counsel advised WND that the Secret Service documents outlining the policies need not be kept out of the press because nothing is marked "classified," "confidential," or "sensitive." If they were considered so, every page would have been appropriately marked.

"This reconfirms my theory from the outset," said Sanders. "After reading the Department of Homeland Security and United States Secret Service Vehicle Pursuit and Use of Force policies, it's quite evident the Department of Justice is covering up the crimes committed against Miriam Carey, an unarmed woman who was not wanted for a felony, or any other crime, for that matter."

Sanders called upon Attorney General Loretta Lynch to give the case its highest priority, with a top-to-bottom review and full public disclosure. "Additionally, we are demanding the United States Congress commence its own parallel investigation into the Department of Justice's handling of the Miriam Carey shooting," he told me.

"The Department of Homeland Security and United States Secret Service policies are just empty words," summed up Sanders. "As established during the Secret Service Oversight Hearings on September 30, 2014, the United States Secret Service is woefully untrained despite a budget well over $800 million."

"In 2012, Secret Service Agents received no basic training course," he continued. "In 2013, they received one training course. With respect to the Uniform Division, they received only one training course in 2012 and 2013."

The attorney went on to say that the management, officers, and other employees of the departments "are simply deliberately indifferent toward upholding the United States Constitution.

"This deliberate indifference resulted in violations of Miriam and her minor child's civil rights."

## 10. POLICE KNEW CAREY WAS NOT A TERRORIST

As we have seen, the only legitimate reason for the Secret Service and the Capitol Police to pursue Carey from the White House would have been if she had posed a threat. Yet, authorities apparently learned almost immediately that the car they were chasing did not belong to someone fitting a terrorist profile, but to a young mother and dental hygienist from Connecticut, according to the Associated Press.[23]

The report, printed in the *New Haven Register* in January 2014, said that when authorities began chasing Carey's vehicle, which had Connecticut license plates, State Police Maj. Louis J. Fusaro Jr., the head of his state's Intelligence Center, led an effort with the Motor Vehicles Department to run the license plates and identify the driver. "Within a matter of minutes of the incident happening, we were able to give back information that was key to the investigation down there," said Fusaro, who is also commander of emergency services and the Office of Counter Terrorism for state police.

"Our job is to validate information, then refer it to the proper agencies for investigation," he told the AP.

Sanders suspects that police received the information about Miriam immediately. That would raise a serious question as to why law enforcement agents shot and killed Carey, rather than attempting to subdue her with nonlethal means.

When were the record searches about Miriam requested? Sanders wondered. Before, during, or after the police chase?

"My law enforcement experience tells me, one or more officers during the police pursuit sent at least one, if not more, messages through the mobile digital computer in their police vehicles to NLETS (National Law Enforcement Telecommunications System, now known as the International Justice and Public Safety Network), and via police radio to their dispatcher, and they received the information about Miriam within seconds, long before she was shot and killed."

## 11. OFFICER CLAIMED TO SHOOT IN SELF-DEFENSE AT A CAR DRIVING AWAY

The first officer to shoot at Carey claimed he pulled the trigger because he feared for his life—even though she was driving *away* from him.

And he shot at her from the back.

Police fired two volleys of gunshots at Carey, first at Garfield Circle, a few blocks west of the Capitol, and then on Constitution Avenue at Second Street and Maryland Avenue, a few blocks east of the Capitol.

Under the heading "Preliminary Investigative Report Concerning the Use of Force" in the police report, a statement read: "The suspect then drove south on the sidewalk of Garfield Circle. In fear for his life, USCP Officer [redacted] discharged his service pistol several times at the suspect's vehicle as she fled the scene."

However, video shot by a news crew at Garfield Circle clearly showed she was driving away from the officers well before they fired.[24] In fact, the audio track of the video demonstrates Carey was no longer even near the officers when the shots are heard.

Additionally, according to the police report, a witness even stated that "as the car [was] driving away the police fire[d] at the vehicle."

It was the job of former U.S. Attorney for the District of Columbia Ronald C. Machen to decide whether to charge officers with using excessive force in the shooting death of Carey. His reasons for not filing charges were not listed in the investigative report obtained by the FOIA request.

Machen's office said little on the Carey case after the announcement on July 10, 2014, that no charges would be filed against officers, other than in a statement that read, in part, "There is more than sufficient evidence to show that under all of the prevailing circumstances at the time, the officers were acting in defense of themselves and others at the time they fired their weapons."

But if officers did fire in self-defense, why were the first shots not fired until Carey was driving away from them?

Officers also claimed they fired at Carey's car in self-defense during the second, and final, volley of shots delivered on Constitution Avenue, where the chase ended and where she was fatally wounded. This is the official version of events and the shooting on Constitution, in the statement issued by the Justice Department on July 10, 2014:

After ignoring multiple commands given by officers who were running towards her vehicle with guns drawn, Ms. Carey revved her engine and then reversed her vehicle and drove directly at a U.S. Capitol Police officer who was approaching Ms. Carey's vehicle from behind. As the U.S. Capitol Police officer ran towards the median to avoid being struck by Ms. Carey's vehicle, he and another officer from the U.S. Secret Service (who also had fired shots at the Garfield Circle location) started firing. The two officers fired nine rounds each. Twenty seconds after Ms. Carey had arrived at the 2nd and Maryland location, her vehicle crashed into the kiosk and came to rest. Ms. Carey was unconscious at this time, and did not get out of the vehicle. No additional rounds were fired by officers after the crash.

But the witness accounts in the police report do not support that official account. Some contradict it.

The first witness said she heard a single gunshot, then looked out the window:

[Redacted] stated that she then heard two (2) to three (3) additional gunshots and observed a black vehicle that was facing west on Maryland Avenue, Northeast, but was in reverse and was backing east on Maryland Avenue, Northeast, until it struck a police booth. [Redacted] reported that after the black vehicle struck the police booth, several officers surrounded the vehicle. [Redacted] advise [*sic*] that as the black vehicle was backing up and before it struck the police booth, there were no police officers near the vehicle.

Note that this witness did not say the car was driving toward an officer, as the DOJ had claimed. In fact, directly contradicting their report that "a U.S. Capitol Police officer . . . was approaching Ms. Carey's vehicle from behind," she said "there were no police officers near the vehicle."

So which officers, do you suppose, were *really* "acting in defense of themselves," as Machen's office asserted?

Apparently, not a single one.

This photo shows just how close Garfield Circle is to the U.S. Capitol. Photo provided by Justice Department.

## 12. OFFICERS ENDANGERED THE PUBLIC WITH GUNFIRE

As tragic as Carey's death was, evidence shows an even greater calamity may have been only narrowly averted.

Officials have never addressed whether officers recklessly endangered the public with the twenty-six bullets they fired on Capitol Hill while trying to stop Carey. But you be the judge:

Eight of the bullets were fired at Garfield Circle, and eighteen were shot at a U.S. Capitol Police guard post in the 100 block of Constitution Avenue, in between the Hart Senate Office building and a lot adjacent to the U.S. Supreme Court.

Garfield Circle is located at the base of Capitol Hill, at the edge of the National Mall and bordered by the Capitol Reflecting Pool, the Capitol Building Tours Ticket Booth, a parking lot and, behind that, the United States Botanic Garden. It is in the very heart of a heavily populated area where tourist buses deposit sightseers with clockwork regularity, and it offers a stunning view of the Capitol, some eight hundred feet up the hill.

Is it not at least marginally plausible that officers were putting the public in grave danger by firing so many times in such crowded areas?

The flags in this evidence photo indicate the location of shell casings from bullets fired at Carey in Garfield Circle. Photo provided by Justice Department.

On that fateful October day, a veritable squadron of police cars followed Carey from the White House to Garfield Circle, where uniformed Secret Service agents and U.S. Capitol Police officers first shot at her.

It's not clear where all the bullets they shot at Garfield Circle landed, but a video shot by a news crew showed the location of

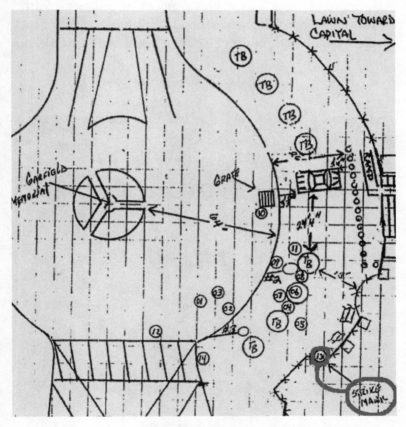

Map provided by Department of Justice.

officers as they fired, on the east side of Garfield Circle.

Carey's car slipped out of view as the shots rang out, then reappeared on the south side of the circle. Officers could be seen shooting in a southerly direction as the car moved first away from them, then from their left to right.

Nothing in the police reports indicated where any of the eight bullets landed, except one. A police map shows a "strike mark," likely indicating where a bullet was found, near a bench on the southeast side of the circle. The words "Strike Mark" can

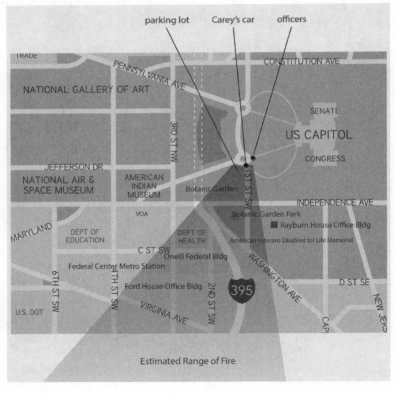

Distances of populated areas from Garfield Circle, including tourist spots, government buildings, and crowded streets.

be seen on the lower right side of the following hand-drawn police map, and the bench just next to it:

The police report said an officer saw two people on a bench. There are two benches on the southeast side of Garfield Circle, so it is not clear just how close the bullet may have come to them, but, it would appear, considerably close. One bench is closer to the east side of the circle. The other, the one closest to the bullet hole, is a few feet away, on the southeast side.

What happened to the seven other bullets? That information is not provided in the Justice Department documents, but it is clear the bullets were fired in the direction of a number of people.

Perhaps miraculously, no bystanders were hurt by gunfire.

Using the available evidence as a guide, the map shows where the officers were, the position of Carey's car, and an estimated range of fire in which the bullets may have traveled.

Following are the distances of populated areas from Garfield Circle, including tourist spots, government buildings, and crowded streets that appear to have been in the line of fire.

- 0 feet to parking lot
- 0 feet to First Street
- 200 feet to Botanic Garden
- 300 feet to Independence Avenue
- 400 feet to Botanic Garden Park
- 400 feet to Rayburn House Office Building
- 500 feet to the Department of Health and Human Services
- 650 feet to the American Veterans Disabled for Life Memorial
- 700 feet to Voice of America

- 800 feet to Interstate 395
- 800 feet to the Thomas P. O'Neill, Jr. Federal Building
- 1,000 feet to the Ford House Office Building
- 1,100 feet to the Federal Center Metro Station
- 1,500 feet to NASA

The people at Garfield Circle obviously had reason to fear for their lives. But so did potentially hundreds of people within range of the gunshots.

The civilians in Garfield Circle were in the greatest immediate danger when officers began firing.

And there were a lot of them.

According to an investigator's handwritten notes of a witness account in the police report, there were "approx 30 people around—no one he knew, appeared to be tourist."

The report further states, "A Capitol Police officer ran up to him with gun drawn and told everyone to get down. Got behind a wall."

The people on the bench were at virtual point-blank range from the officers.

Everyone else in Garfield Circle must have also been in extreme danger. The police report said one such person, who was close enough to see the people on the bench, "dove on the ground for protection" when he heard the gunshots.

Another nearby witness told police "she fell to the ground once the shooting began."

People in the parking lot adjacent to the circle were not much farther away, and, possibly, also in the line of fire.

At least one person in the parking lot ducked when the shots rang out. According to the police report, that witness, who had come to town to see a hockey game, "dropped behind a vehicle" when the officers fired at Carey's Infiniti.

Just behind the parking lot is the Botanic Garden, a popular tourist destination. To the east of the garden is First Street, which runs just three hundred feet to heavily trafficked Independence Avenue.

On the corner of First and Independence is the Rayburn Office Building, the workplace of 169 members of Congress and thousands of their staff members and other federal employees.

To the east of Rayburn is where Interstate 395 ducks under Capitol Hill through a tunnel.

To the west of that, and right behind the Botanic Garden, are the Department of Health and Human Services and the Voice of America office buildings.

Behind those buildings are the O'Neill Federal Building, a subway station, the Ford House Office Building, and NASA.

So, the officers shot in the direction of the people on the bench, the Rayburn House offices, First Street, Independence Avenue, a parking lot, the U.S. Botanic Garden, an interstate highway, and the Department of Health. They were all in the immediate vicinity, and in danger.

Yet the officers' own lives were not in danger from Carey.

The underlying question: Were they justified in firing?

More specifically, were police justified in endangering the public to stop an unarmed, suburban mother from going on her way—all because she refused to stop for an unidentified man wearing civilian clothes and carrying a cooler, who threw a bike rack in front of her car?

The Department of Justice has yet to answer.

## 13. CAREY WAS SHOT IN THE BACK

Miriam Carey was shot in the back.

Three times.

And once in the side of the head from the rear.

As shown in the previous section, officers shot at her a total of twenty-six times, hitting her five times.

Carey's autopsy report was prepared by Dr. Nikki Mourtzinos of the Office of the Chief Medical Examiner for the District of Columbia. She found no drugs or alcohol in Carey's system. What she did find was plenty of bullet holes.

According to the autopsy report, one bullet hit Carey in the arm.[25]

This photo, taken from the spot where Carey was killed, shows how close it was to the U.S. Supreme Court, seen behind the police car. Photo provided by Justice Department.

Three struck her in the back.

A shot to the head, under her left ear, seemed to have been the fatal blow. That bullet also came from the rear, as it traveled back to front, and left to right, through her skull and into her brain.

So who shot these bullets, and where?

Two Secret Service officers and a Capitol Police officer fired a total of eight shots at Carey's moving car at Garfield Circle. A Secret Service officer and a Capitol Police officer each fired nine shots at Carey on Constitution Avenue.

Carey's car, with three bullet holes in the passenger door. Photo provided by Justice Department.

Photos of Carey's bullet-ridden car obtained from the DOJ by a FOIA request show it was struck numerous times on the driver's side from both the front and the rear and three times in the passenger door.

Some of the holes in the back of the car may have been from bullets fired at the first shooting scene, Garfield Circle, when Carey departed the circle and drove her car directly away from officers, heading south.

The rods inside the bullet holes pictured here indicate the angle at which the bullets entered the car. Photo provided by Justice Department.

One of the bullets fired from the front came from the side. Photo provided by Justice Department.

This photo shows some of the bullet holes from the side and rear. Photo provided by Justice Department.

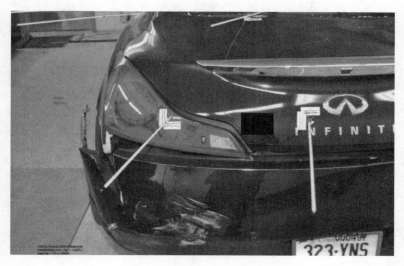

Bullet holes in the rear. Photo provided by Justice Department.

A close-up of bullet holes in the front. Photo provided by Justice Department.

Photo provided by U.S. Attorney.

Photo provided by U.S. Attorney.

After driving directly away from officers, Carey followed the circle, moving from the officers' left to right, exposing her passenger door to their fire. That is likely when the bullet holes were made in the passenger door.

The holes in the front of the car were all made by bullets fired at the second shooting scene, on Constitution, which is the only location where an officer fired at her from the front.

Officers fired on her from both the front and the back on Constitution.

The Justice Department said investigators do not believe Carey was hit by any of the rounds at Garfield.

The coroner said the head shot likely killed Carey.

Still photos from video shot at the scene on Constitution

do show an officer in position to fire a shot that would match the angle of the bullet that struck Carey in the head, as seen in the photo on the previous page.

That is why the Carey family attorney has an alternate theory.

Sanders believes the shot that struck Carey in the head was fired as officers moved to their left and fired at her car as it departed Garfield Circle. Though the shot proved to be fatal, he speculated, adrenaline allowed her to continue driving up Constitution Avenue to Maryland Avenue and Second Street.

He insisted that such a scenario is quite plausible and that something similar happens more often than people realize.

"First, despite popular belief, people can receive a fatal injury and bleed out over the course of twenty-four hours," he told me. "Remember, President Lincoln survived approximately nine hours after being shot in his head. That was in the late 1800s."

"We probably see a dozen gunshot wounds to the head each year where people survive. [Lincoln] had a non-fatal injury by 2007 standards," surgeon and director of the Shock Trauma Center Thomas M. Scalea told the *Washington Post* in 2007. That article claimed that Lincoln might have even survived the gunshot wound if he'd had access to modern medicine.[26]

### 14. A BULLET MAY HAVE HIT CAREY'S CHILD

According to the police report, Carey's thirteen-month-old child was "covered in glass and blood" when she was finally taken from the car following her mother's shooting.

Whose blood? That's not quite clear.

Was the child badly injured? That's not clear, either.

This is what the Capitol Police officer who removed the child from the car told investigators:

Officer [redacted] said when the shots stopped he ran toward the suspect's vehicle and noticed a small child in the back seat in a car seat. Officer [redacted] said the driver was unresponsive and he signaled to the other officers there was a child in the car. Officer [redacted] said he broke the car window and pulled the child from the car. Officer [redacted] said the child was covered in glass and blood. Officer [redacted] said he wiped the child off and checked her for any injuries. Officer [redacted] said he rushed the child indoors and had a nurse treat the child. Officer [redacted] said he rode in the ambulance with the child to Children's Hospital.

The report said he "checked her for any injuries." It did not say whether he found any.

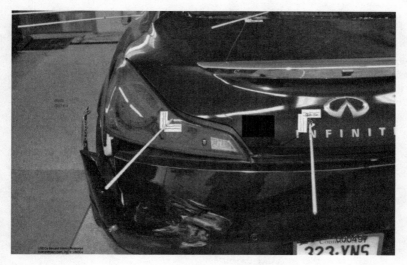

Photo provided by Justice Department.

Looking at the evidence photo of the bullet holes in Carey's car, one can't help but wonder, how in the world did a toddler in the backseat survive that barrage of bullets?

And did she really escape unscathed, as authorities insisted?

The evidence shows just how close federal officers came to killing that little girl.

And it raises questions about whether she was hurt, perhaps seriously.

The rods in the photographs on these pages show the location of the bullet holes and the angles of the shots fired by federal officers at the front and the back of the car in the onslaught that killed Carey.

Following their trajectories produces a chilling mental image of bullets whizzing past a terrified baby—whose mother's gruesome death she would then witness right in front of her face.

Somehow, her daughter survived, thanks to her being on the right side of the car, instead of the left.

Photo provided by Justice Department.

Photo provided by Justice Department.

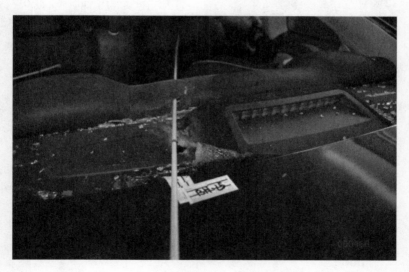

Photo provided by Justice Department.

But in the close-ups on the previous page, the rod on the right shows how one shot came within an inch or two of the child's car seat—well within reach of a dangling left arm.

Photo provided by Justice Department.

The Justice Department said the child "was not seriously injured." But look at this photo of the car seat:

Both photos (to the left and on page 77) show shattered glass strewn all around the child seat. Even more ominously, the photo on this page appears to show blood smears or spatter on the side of the child seat.

The side where the bullet hit.

And where her left arm would have been.

The evidence indicates it was entirely possible that a bullet hit the child. One nearly hit her child seat. The child was covered in blood. There was also blood on the child seat, on the side where a bullet could easily have hit her.

All of this evidence raises serious questions:

- Was the child covered in her mother's blood or her own? Both?

- Was the child injured?

- If so, how seriously?

- Was she shot?

- If so, how badly was she wounded?

- Did she suffer cuts from flying glass?

- Did she suffer any other physical trauma?

- What about psychological trauma?

- What is the effect on a toddler who witnesses her own mother shot to death in front of her face?

Photo provided by Justice Department.

## 15. THE CHILD WAS HOSPITALIZED

The police report said: "The officers also observed a child, who was conscious and breathing at the time, seated in the rear of the vehicle. The child was immediately removed from the vehicle and provided medical attention."

Neither that statement nor the earlier one, from the officer who retrieved the child and accompanied her to the hospital, said whether she was injured or not. But one implied the need for immediate medical attention. The other said the officer "rushed the child indoors and had a nurse treat the child."

- What kind of immediate medical attention was "provided"?

- What were the child's specific injuries?

- How severe were those injuries?

- What did the nurse do?

- What treatment did she receive there?

Not only was the officer compelled to get the child immediate medical attention, he also found it necessary to accompany her to the hospital. Both admirable actions, by an officer who showed exemplary concern for the child's welfare. Perhaps it was just an overabundance of precaution. But why such evident urgency?

Was the child seriously hurt? If she had been injured, wouldn't the Carey family know? Did they see any wounds or scars during subsequent visits with the girl?

No, because they had extremely limited access to the child after the shooting.

A court awarded custody of the child to her father, Carey's former boyfriend, from whom she was estranged. The child's aunts and grandmother did not even see her until months after the shooting.

"Oh, they only saw her once or twice for a very, very brief time in the presence of the father in public places. The visits

Photo provided by Justice Department.

occurred in or around spring 2014," Sanders told me.

In October 2015, Sanders told me the Carey family hadn't physically seen the child for almost a year. "Nor were they ever in the position to ascertain whether she was injured," he added. "Nor were they ever informed by the father or the child's lawyer handling the estate of her physical or mental status."

"For that matter," he continued, "other than me trying to keep the legal claims alive (on behalf of the family) and investigating Miriam's death, no one, including the father, did anything for her legally or otherwise."

The headlines on October 3, 2013, were about Miriam Carey. Most major publications mistakenly reported that she was shot after attempting to ram her way into the White House.

Largely lost in the shuffle was the fate of a forgotten little victim, the daughter who lost her mother.

## 16. WITNESSES VERSUS OFFICERS

That the official account of the shooting death provided by the Department of Justice differs significantly from accounts provided by the civilian witnesses in the police report is well established.

Contrary to the DOJ version of events, which you read earlier:

- not one of five witnesses said Carey's car was driving toward an officer

- four of the five witnesses did not mention her car traveling in reverse

- three did not say if her car was even in motion when shots were fired

- three did not state that an officer was near the car when shots were fired

- one witness said the car was moving back and forth, suggesting it was stuck

- another witness said it was stuck; then officers fired a barrage of bullets and killed the unarmed mother

Let's take a closer look at what each of the witnesses said:

### WITNESS 1

This woman was at work when she heard a single gunshot, then looked out the window.

According to the police report:

[Redacted] stated that she then heard two (2) to three (3) additional gunshots and observed a black vehicle that was facing west on Maryland Avenue, Northeast, but was in reverse and was backing east on Maryland Avenue, Northeast, until it struck a police booth. [Redacted] reported that after the black vehicle struck the police booth, several officers surrounded the vehicle. [Redacted] advise[d] that as the black vehicle was backing up and before it struck the police booth, there were no police officers near the vehicle.

This witness did not say the car was driving toward an officer.

She did not say officers were near the car when she heard shots.

She did say the car traveled in reverse but she contradicted the Justice Department account that Carey "reversed her vehicle and drove directly at a U.S. Capitol Police officer who was approaching Ms. Carey's vehicle from behind" because she said "that as the black vehicle was backing up and before it struck the police booth, there were no police officers near the vehicle."

In other words, she does not support the official contention that Carey was moving toward and threatening an officer.

## WITNESS 2

A cab driver traveling west on Constitution Avenue said he saw police cars and heard sirens.

[Redacted] states he noticed the car trying to avoid the barracks and go up on the median curb. The car continued and he then heard about two to three shots. He saw an officer with his gun drawn but couldn't say whether he saw the officer shot [sic]. He duck [sic] and when he held his head up the black was surrounded by officer [sic].

- He did not say the car drove toward an officer.

- He did not say the car was in reverse.

- He did not say officers were near the car until after shots were fired.

- He did not actually say if the car was in motion when shots were fired.

## WITNESS 3
This woman reported that she heard sirens and a "loud boom, like a collision."

> [Redacted] observed police cars surrounding a vehicle and gun-fire. [Redacted] then saw officers running and police vehicles running. [Redacted] thought she saw an officer pull a child from the vehicle. [Redacted] saw officers with their weapons drawn and officers discharge their weapons at the vehicle.

This same witness told CNN she saw the black car hit what appeared to be a trash can and a police car, "which turned the car sideways. There's a little window booth where the policemen stand, and the security guards, who guard us every day on the corner, and at that time her car was surrounded by police and a lot of armed men and that's where the gunfire began."

- She did not say the car was in reverse.

- She did not say the car drove toward an officer.

- She did not say the car was moving when officers fired.

WITNESS 4

This witness also did not hear gunshots until after police cars surrounded Carey's car:

> The black vehicle drove over the median and began traveling west bound. One of the police vehicles pulled approximately ten feet behind the black vehicle. Another of the police cars pulled approximately ten feet in front of the black vehicle. At this time all of the police officers exited their vehicles and began issuing commands to stop and to exit the vehicle. The black vehicle continued to move forwards and back ward [*sic*] as the officers gave the commands. Detective [redacted] asked Mrs. [redacted] if she had any difficulty hearing the officers and she stated that she did not. Those commands were given verbally and over a loud speaker [*sic*]. The driver's side window was down a couple of inches according to Mrs. [redacted]. It is Mrs. [redacted] belief that the officers were standing a couple of feet away from the black vehicle at this time.
>
> Mrs. [redacted] states that she heard two gun shots that she believed came from the black vehicle. After the first two gunshots Ms. [*sic*] [redacted] heard numerous additional gunshots. At this time everything became quiet.

- She did say police cars were positioned in front of, and behind, Carey's car.

- She did not say the car drove toward an officer.

- She did not say the car was traveling in reverse.

- She said the car continued to move forward and backward.

WITNESS 5

A fifth witness? There is vivid description of the shooting by someone who apparently was close enough to see it very clearly. But, perhaps curiously, his account was not included in the witness statements in the FOIA information turned over by the DOJ. This is what the *Washington Post* reported on October 3, 2013, the day of the shooting:

> 46-year-old tourist Edmund Ofori-Attah was walking toward the Hart building to ask if it was open for tours. With most of Washington's top attractions shut down, touring an office building sounded better than nothing.
>
> Then he saw a black car whiz past. It abruptly turned left, as if to make a U-turn, and lodged itself on a grassy divide.
>
> "That's where it got pinned," he said. "At that point, we heard five to six rounds of gunfire and my wife and I dropped to the ground. We were hoping not to get in the way of a stray bullet—we just lay down as low as possible. We even smelled the gunpowder in the air."[27]

- He did not say Carey's car was driving toward an officer.

- He did not say her car was traveling in reverse.

- He did not say her car was in motion when shots were fired.

- He did not say an officer was near the car when shots were fired.

- In fact, he told the *Post* that the car was lodged on the median.

Pinned.
As in, unable to move.

Stuck. Defenseless.
Only then did he hear gunshots.
After the car was immobilized.
With an unarmed woman and her child inside.

Carey's car came to rest against the guardhouse on Constitution Avenue at Maryland Avenue and Second Street. Photo provided by Justice Department.

If Ofori-Attah's account is to be believed, the killing of Carey would seem to have been a summary execution of a trapped and defenseless victim.

Still photographs from video released by the Justice Department could be seen as backing up the official contention that Carey drove in reverse after her way forward was blocked, and that her car was indeed in motion when officers fired.

But even then, the sequence of events is problematic because there is still no evidence that officers were threatened or had no other choice but to shoot.

In the photos we see an officer in front of Carey and another behind her. Yet even if the photos indicate she drove in reverse, it does not mean she was driving at the officer, but only in his direction, as he seemed to have easily moved out of her way and off to her side. And without seeing Carey's car in motion, and without knowing exactly when the shots were fired, it is impossible to tell for certain what happened and when.

Here is the sequence of photographs.

This one shows Carey crossing the median after the raised barriers in front of her had blocked her path:

Photo provided by Justice Department.

Carey's path is then blocked by a squad car:

Photo provided by Justice Department.

Officers appear in front and back of Carey's car with guns drawn, possibly firing. Their positions would be consistent with bullet holes in Carey's car:

Photo provided by Justice Department.

Photo provided by Justice Department.

As seen in the photo above, Carey does seem to be going in reverse, but again, the officer seems to easily move out of her way.

The officer who was behind her is now to her side, in position to deliver a shot consistent with what the autopsy described as the mortal wound:

Photo provided by Justice Department.

Neither officer appears to be in danger.
But Carey was done.

# 3

# MISSING EVIDENCE

THE AMOUNT OF INFORMATION redacted, or censored, in response to my FOIA requests was substantial. Entire pages were blacked out. Critically, there was not one statement from any of the officers who shot at Carey. Crucial video from the White House and the site of the killing were missing. Dozens of witness statements were missing. So were the transcripts of many witness statements. Many firsthand accounts were replaced by paraphrased versions made by investigators.

These were not minor omissions and this was not business as usual. This appeared to be a concerted effort to hide the truth.

The Metropolitan Police Department (MPD) did not turn over crime-scene photos, but the DOJ did, including some in the form of stills from the surveillance videos shot at the guard posts at the White House and on Constitution, but not the videos themselves. The DOJ also turned over a number of DVDs with traffic-camera videos, but they revealed nothing but shots of ordinary traffic.

Most important was the absence of any mention of the results of the investigation. There is no mention of what evidence supposedly exonerated the officers and why their superiors chose not to file charges against them. Both the DOJ and MPD failed to turn over any findings from the investigation, but it was the DOJ's response to the FOIA request that eventually would reveal that such findings did, indeed, exist.

We will explore that in depth, but first, let's take a look at the items authorities failed to provide, one by one:

- redacted information
- security camera videos
- police radio recordings
- ballistics and forensics reports
- police statements
- clothes
- witness statements
- investigation findings

The DOJ, like the MPD, failed to turn over any findings from the investigation. But, it was the DOJ's response to the FOIA request that eventually would reveal that such findings did, indeed, exist. Let's take a look at the items the MPD failed to provide, one by one:

### REDACTED INFORMATION
Redacted material in an official document is information that literally has been blacked out. A redaction is a form of censorship.

There are legitimate reasons to redact material in an official document.

When used properly, a redaction can protect the innocent. When used improperly, it can protect the guilty.

In response to WND's successful FOIA appeal to the Washington mayor's office, an MPD officer personally handed over a DVD copy of the police report on the investigation into the death of Miriam Carey. Just before that, an attorney in the Washington, D.C., mayor's office told me over the phone that the only redactions were names, in order to protect privacy.

Turns out, much more than names was redacted.

The report was riddled with blacked-out sections and missing information.

This is one of the 322 pages of that report:

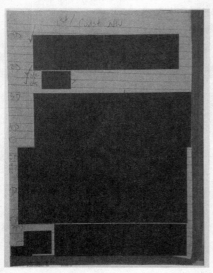

Photo provided by Washington Metropolitan
Police Department.

The image on page 94 was not an isolated example:

- 12 pages in the report were entirely blacked out

- 15 pages were mostly blacked out

- 22 pages were partially blacked out

And that tally does not include the numerous blacked-out sections and pages that appear to have been redacted solely to protect personal information that might identify witnesses.

Some of the blacked-out pages just included a heading marked "Evidence." Others had only a date.

Some, like the image on the next page, had just the word *Detective* handwritten at the top of a piece of notebook paper, indicating they were either notes or statements from an officer.

One had an entire e-mail reply blacked out.

Some of the redactions appeared to be descriptions of videos.

What did Sanders make of all of the redactions in the report?

"If there was information that would have helped the police, they would have been all too happy to release it," he told me. "That means the information would have helped the Carey family's legal position."

But that missing information was hardly all that was omitted.

Photo provided by Washington Metropolitan Police Department.

Photo provided by Washington Metropolitan Police Department.

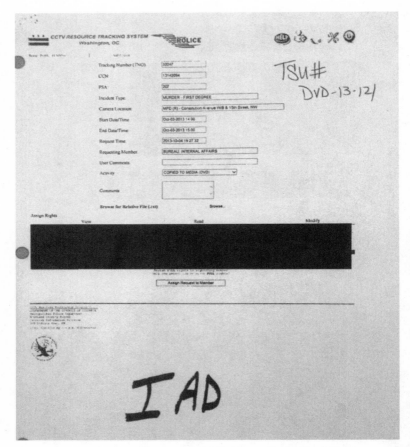

Photo provided by Washington Metropolitan Police Department.

### SECURITY CAMERA VIDEOS

Based on the documents in the report, it appears police used video from ten security cameras in their investigation.

No security camera video was included in the material turned over by the MPD or the DOJ.

Police cruiser dash-cam videos also were not provided.

Traffic camera video was not included in the FOIA material provided by the MPD.

However, the Justice Department did provide fourteen DVDs of traffic camera video in response to its FOIA request, but the footage shows almost nothing but normal traffic.

One video briefly shows Carey's car from a distance as it departed Garfield Circle, but nothing revealing. However, another video that shows nothing but normal traffic may be quite revealing precisely for what it does not show.

The video in question shows normal traffic on Pennsylvania Avenue between the White House and the Capitol during the time frame in which Carey drove that route. What it does *not* show is any sign of a high-speed chase.

That directly contradicts the DOJ's claim that Carey "drove down Pennsylvania Avenue at speeds estimated at 40–80 mph." And it backs up the *Washington Post*'s insinuation that apparently no such high-speed chase took place, because Carey averaged 19.5 miles per hour along that route.[1]

Of crucial importance is what security videos would show as Carey

- entered and departed the White House guard post

- was chased by officers

- was shot at by officers at Garfield Circle

- was shot by officers on Constitution Avenue

The nation's capital is blanketed by security camera coverage. Sanders estimates that ninety cameras recorded at least some of what happened to Carey. Surely the White House guard post at Fifteenth and E Streets had cameras covering every square inch.

Garfield Circle is just inside the edge of the U.S. Capitol grounds, at the base of Capitol Hill. It is most likely covered by cameras.

The Capitol Police guard post at Constitution Avenue and Second Street is surrounded by cameras, including some visibly attached to the shack.

An in-person investigation revealed the presence of at least seven security cameras in positions to capture video of the Carey shooting at that final scene. The incident was also likely captured by police cruiser dash cams.

The existence of video of the shooting on Constitution was confirmed a few weeks after the incident by merely approaching the guard shack where Carey was shot, about a block from the

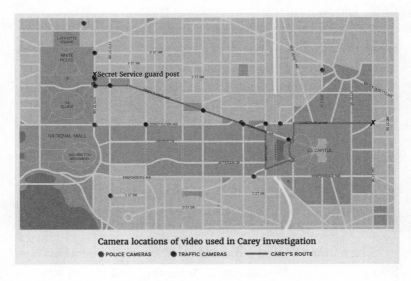

Camera locations of video used in Carey investigation

● POLICE CAMERAS   ● TRAFFIC CAMERAS   ——— CAREY'S ROUTE

Capitol dome, and asking a police officer on duty a few simple questions:

"If a major crime, such as a rape or murder, were to happen within blocks of the Capitol, would there be video of it?"

"Oh yeah," he answered, nodding vigorously.

"What about the shooting of Miriam Carey; is there video of that?"

"Yes," he said without hesitation, while adding he had not seen it personally.

Apparently no one has seen it, other than perhaps a few select members of law enforcement.

The DOJ did release some stills from video of the shooting on Constitution, shown in chapter 2. But, for the reasons cited in that chapter, it is impossible to know what really happened there without seeing the actual video.

One document in the police report stated, "CCTV (closed circuit TV) Footage has been obtained by: [redacted]."

According to the following transcript, the Secret Service, Capitol Police, and the MPD all had copies of "all evidence reports, audio/video interviews and surveillance footage collected during the course of this investigation":

On July 30, 2014, Agent [redacted] provided a copy of all evidence reports, audio/video interviews and surveillance footage collected during the course of this investigation to Sergeant [redacted] of the USCP. On that same date, all copies of video footage provided by the USCP that captured the area in which this incident occurred was turned over to Sergeant of the USCP1. On July 31, 2014, Agent [redacted] provided a copy of all evidence reports and audio/video interviews collected during the course of this investigation to Special Agent [redacted] of the USSS. The MPD only provided copies of the video footage of this incident to the USAO (U.S. Attorney's Office) and no other copies were produced by MPD.

Police departments in major cities such as Philadelphia and Las Vegas have released videos of officer-involved shootings before their investigations were complete. In contrast, the Secret Service, Capitol Police, Washington Metro Police, and the U.S. Attorney withheld virtually all details of the shooting, including video, from Carey's family and from the public, even after concluding their investigation.

Why? What were they trying to hide?

What could that missing video have shown?

"It would have confirmed my hypothesis the White House guards were not paying attention and she drove through the area because they failed to maintain their post," said Sanders. "And all they did was play catch up and then overcompensated by trying to stop her and then pursuing her."

Sanders also insisted to me the video would reveal what actually happened as Carey tried to lawfully leave the White House guard post and what happened when the off-duty agent tried to stop her.

"It would have shown that she tried to avoid him. It would have shown that he did not show his badge, his identification as an officer. It's now established he never identified himself," he told me. "As a matter of fact, if he did identify himself, I guarantee you they would have included his statement and it would have said, 'I identified myself in a loud and clear voice.'"

There was no statement from that officer included in the report.

There were also no statements from the four officers who fired shots at Carey.

There was just the summary of what an officer told investigators when he claimed he fired on Carey at Garfield Circle out of "fear for his life," even though it is clear from video shot by a news crew that he fired only after she was driving away from him and well out of his way.

Sanders contends that the actual statements from officers would have been invaluable. "They would have given us the basis of why they believe they had the right to fire on her vehicle," he said. "And I think the reason *why* they didn't turn it over is because it didn't favor them. It would have revealed they had no legal basis for shooting. If the missing data would have supported their legal position and shown why they had a legal right to use force, they would have released it."

Sanders believes the definitive explanation as to how Carey ended up dead will be revealed when law enforcement finally releases security camera video of her encounter with officers at the White House guard gate.

## POLICE RADIO RECORDINGS

No recordings or transcripts of radio transmissions during the pursuit and shooting of Carey were provided in the FOIA material. Also not provided were transcripts of computer transmissions (instant messaging) between squad cars and police headquarters.

In an e-mail, Sanders told me police should have turned over "all radio transmissions and/or mobile digital communications (mobile digital terminals and/or other cellular technologies) from the Secret Service and Capitol Police, other government agency or provider (E-911 responders, etc.) communicating information about Miriam Carey and the pursuit." The missing radio recordings and transcripts of those conversations would have shown definitively whether the Secret Service officer at the White House guard gate who said he saw Carey's infant daughter in the backseat of her car informed police of the child's presence.

As mentioned in chapter 2, some have questioned whether an antiquated police radio system may have contributed to the deadly chaos. NBC News reported an alleged failure in radio "interoperability" that left Secret Service officers unable to communicate with Capitol Police during the chase.[2]

Five days after the killing of Carey, Sen. Susan Collins (R-ME) expressed alarm that a faulty radio system might have been an issue. "If these communication failures are in fact accurate, it is extremely concerning that this problem still has not been resolved after years of experience with such situations, as well as billions of dollars spent to resolve our weaknesses in interoperable communications systems," said the former chairwoman and ranking member of the Senate Homeland Security and Governmental Affairs Committee.[3]

Former NYPD sergeant Valarie Carey told me problems with police radios could have been a factor in her sister's death. But it struck her that a bigger issue may have been inexperience on the part of the officers who killed Miriam. She believed the officers may have panicked because they had never experienced such a situation.

"The more experienced an officer is, the better equipped that officer is to address the situation, even if there had been a problem with radio contact," she said. "If someone can't decide when to take someone's life, they should not be put in that position."

On December 19, 2013, two and a half months after Carey was killed, and after eight years and at a cost of more than $100 million, Capitol Police finally replaced their three-decades-old radios with a modernized, encrypted digital radio system.

## BALLISTICS AND FORENSICS REPORTS

I filed a FOIA request with MPD for the ballistics and forensics reports but never received a reply to multiple inquiries regarding the status of that request.

The Justice Department and MPD responses to FOIA requests for the full police report filed later did not include a ballistics or a forensics report.

Sanders told me that was not standard for a police report.

"There was no ballistics report. No testing of the group of responding officers' firearms, only the four identified. No analysis of the recovered .357 cartridges from, presumably, Miriam's body."

The former NYPD officer said that while the autopsy report showed how many times Carey was shot and the probable cause of death, a forensics report also would have had multiple eyewitness accounts and an explanation as to why police believed deadly force was necessary to subdue her while she was unarmed.

## CLOTHES

Carey's clothes apparently did not make it to the medical examiner's office, just her naked body.

There is no mention of what happened to them in any police document.

Sanders said it appeared her clothes were lost and that not examining them would violate standard procedure. Unfortunately, much could have been determined from examining gunshot residue on her clothing, perhaps even confirming the location of the fatal shot.

### POLICE STATEMENTS

The police report said that four officers fired shots at Carey, two from the Capitol Police and two from the Secret Service.

Not one statement from those officers was in the report. Their names were also redacted.

Sanders told me those names should have been released because "police officers do not have a right of privacy as indicated by the case law. The *Washington Post* had an article about that very issue."

Judging by the police report, it appears three of the shooters gave statements. It is unclear if the fourth, a Secret Service officer, was interviewed.

Sanders said by law, in a criminal inquiry all four should have given statements.

According to the Investigative File Report, "Agent 11 [redacted] obtained video-taped interviews from Sergeant [redacted] and Officer [redacted] of the [redacted] United States Secret Service Police, Uniformed Division, (redacted.) A ent [*sic*] [redacted] also obtained a statement from [redacted] United States Capitol Police, [redacted]."

There is no mention of a statement by the second Capitol Police officer.

The report also said handwritten notes had been collected from six detectives and one sergeant, but it does not say which departments they served. All of those names were also redacted.

The information in what appears to be copies of those notes is almost entirely redacted.

There is a mention of one officer who fired a weapon at Garfield Circle, and a secondhand account of his statement: "Officer [redacted] of the USCP discharged his service pistol several times at Ms. Carey's vehicle as she fled the scene. Ms. Carey continued to drive northbound on First Street, Northeast, and then eastbound in the 100 block of Constitution Avenue, Northeast." However, the report also confirmed that more than one officer fired a weapon at Garfield Circle.

The report also said both a Secret Service officer and a Capitol Police officer fired at her on Constitution, and gave brief, secondhand accounts of their statements:

> UD and USCP pursued the suspect vehicle to 2nd Street and Constitution Avenue, Northeast where Carey stopped the suspect vehicle abruptly, and then turned left and drove over a median strip. Carey then drove in reverse in the 200 block of Maryland Avenue, Northeast, during which time, Carey again refused to stop. At this point, officers from both USSS-UD and USCP fired several rounds into the suspect vehicle, striking Carey.

## WITNESS STATEMENTS

An astonishing thirty-eight witness accounts are missing from the police report. The report stated:

> There were seventy-two (72) witnesses interviewed regarding this incident and their statements were captured by audio and/or video recordings. Copies of the aforementioned

recordings were turned over to the USAO for review. Copies of the aforementioned audio and video recordings are stored in the main case file at the Technical Support Unit (TSU) located at the IAD.

Of those seventy-two witness statements, only thirty-four were in the materials provided to me.

Some of the witness statements were blank. One just said the interview was recorded.

Seven of them said, "See video for entire statement."

No videos of witness statements were turned over.

"It's hard to tell because it looks like they really only have statements from maybe five people. There are probably a good five statements, six or seven, tops," noted Sanders, adding, "A lot of those statements are duplicates."

Additionally, none of the actual transcripts of interviews in the witnesses' own words were provided, just paraphrased versions in what the former NYPD officer described as "cop talk."

"That's telling, in and of, itself," said Sanders. "But even their paraphrases, which try to imply the shooting was justified, show that it was not."

### INVESTIGATION FINDINGS

The most important missing evidence does not come from the crime scene.

It is not evidence about the actions of Carey.

It is evidence about the actions of police.

It is evidence investigators failed to provide.

Where is the evidence that the deadly shooting of Carey was justified?

Where is the document with findings that show why the shooting was justified?

Where is the document that details the reasons officers were not charged with manslaughter due to recklessness and/or incompetence?

Where is the analysis of the evidence?

Where are the conclusions based on that evidence and analysis?

Where is anything that says why this was not unjustifiable homicide?

Nowhere in the police report is it explained why officers used deadly force.

Nowhere is it examined whether officers followed the policy of their agencies.

Nowhere is it explained how and why Carey posed a threat justifying deadly force.

There was simply no analysis provided as to why Carey was shot.

There also was no analysis, or even discussion, of why criminal charges were not warranted.

There was not even any evidence that investigators did reach the conclusion the deadly shooting of Carey was justified.

There is nothing but a blue wall of silence on whether the killing of Carey was justified.

That's why Sanders says he believes there was no real attempt to obtain justice for Carey. The officers were simply cleared of wrongdoing based on what was vaguely labeled "more than sufficient evidence" that they were acting in self-defense when they killed the single mother. The *Washington Post* reported the U.S. attorney's office "would not detail what that evidence is."

Unexplained is how officers could have credibly claimed to have fired in self-defense as Carey was driving away from them.

The FOIA requests specifically sought the final report and the findings of the shooting investigation. I asked Sanders if, in his experience as a former NYPD officer, such findings, along with an analysis of whether a shooting was justified, were normally included in a police report.

"Usually you have some findings because every major police department does have a shooting team," he replied. "And a shooting team not only looks at the weapons discharges but also makes sure the discharges are within department guidelines. That wasn't done here."

In fact, he said, so much was missing, and so much police work apparently was never done, that he believed the police never actually conducted a real investigation, or even compiled a final report, at all.

His assessment of the report?

"It's nothing. It's not worth the paper it's written on."

The attorney said it was telling that the police report included legal definitions of terrorism obtained from a Cornell University website. He believes that shows that authorities were desperate to find a definition of terrorism, after the fact, that they could use to justify the shooting.

"We still don't know what the legal basis is for the claim her killing was justified or why they tried to stop her in the first place."

Sanders paused, then with a touch of bewilderment concluded: "They had to say something. They had to say why they discharged their weapons. We still don't know that."

# 4

# JUSTICE DENIED

"JUSTICE DELAYED IS JUSTICE denied," said British prime minister William E. Gladstone in 1868. That is no less true today.

The road to justice for Miriam Carey and her family has been long, tortured, and blocked by government stonewalls. The following timeline demonstrates the protracted nature of this case.

- OCTOBER 3, 2013: Carey shot and killed.

- OCTOBER 3, 2013: Police launch investigation.

- JULY 10, 2014: Justice Department announces no criminal charges would be filed against officers.

- AUGUST 4, 2014: FOIA requests filed with MPD and the Justice Department requesting Carey case evidence and final report.

- AUGUST 24, 2014: FOIA deadline passes with neither Justice Department nor MPD response.

- OCTOBER 17, 2014: FOIA request denied by MPD.

- DECEMBER 8, 2014: MPD FOIA appeal filed with Washington, D.C., mayor's office.

- APRIL 4, 2015: MPD FOIA appeal granted by Washington, D.C., mayor's office.

- MAY 4-17, 2015: Five-part series on MPD FOIA published by WND revealing contradictions between witness and police accounts, and showing how much evidence was missing.

- MARCH 19, 2015: Justice Department says FOIA request waiting to be assigned and processed by a paralegal.

- APRIL 14, 2015: Judicial Watch and WND sue Justice Department to compel FOIA compliance.

- SEPTEMBER 9, 2015: Justice Department begins rolling production of FOIA documents.

- OCTOBER 25-27, 2015: Three-part series published by WND explaining many contradictions in FOIA documents and showing how much evidence still missing.

- FEBRUARY 12, 2016: Justice Department deadline to explain missing documents to judge.

- 2013-2016: 40 investigative stories on the Carey case published by WND; 112 total stories published on the Carey case by WND.

The bottom line: the Justice Department has refused to release the final report allegedly concluding that the Carey shooting was justified.

However, what police and investigators did not provide speaks volumes. And it doesn't speak well for them.

## 1. A SMOKING GUN

The Washington Metro Police Department report contained a smoking-gun e-mail chain in which investigators for the U.S. Attorney's Office for the District of Columbia (part of the Justice Department) and the police discuss the difficulties in releasing the findings of their investigation to the public.

There are four reasons why this e-mail chain is a smoking gun demonstrating that authorities covered up the truth of the Carey case:

1. The e-mails show the findings would have exposed officers and their departments to a lawsuit.

2. The Justice Department tried to hide the existence of the e-mails.

3. The Justice Department tried to hide the existence of the findings.

4. The Justice Department is trying to prevent the release of the findings.

The e-mail exchange that follows shows that officials did not want to release a final report, or an analysis of whether the shooting was justified, because that might have revealed something that could have exposed them to litigation.

Consequently, Metro Police apparently did not do a report with any conclusions based on its investigation.

Indeed, in one of these e-mails, MPD assistant chief of

police of the Internal Affairs Bureau Michael Anzallo bluntly states: "We will not be doing a final report."

This is the e-mail exchange with Anzallo, initiated by someone (name redacted) in the United States Attorney's Office, District of Columbia (USADC):

Tuesday, May 27, 2014 11:12 AM

From: [redacted] (USADC)

Sent: Tuesday, May 27, 2014 11:12 AM

To: Anzallo, Michael (MPD)

Cc: Dixon, George (MPD)

Subject: Capitol case

Hi. My memo is now with Ron, so we are nearer to a decision in this case. I just saw [redacted] and he [redacted] mentioned [redacted] that [redacted] he needed to do the final report if we decline. I told him that I thought that doing so would put MPD right in the middle of the upcoming litigation, and that, because your Use of Force policy is different from USCPs, which is different from [redacted] USSS, that might create a big issue if [redacted] IAD renders an opinion as to whether this particular shooting was justified. Just my thoughts . . .


Tuesday, May 27, 2014 11:16 AM

From: Anzallo, Michael (MPD)

To: [redacted] USADC

Cc: Dixon, George (MPD)

Subject: RE: Capitol case

That is correct. We will not be doing a final report. We would like to include your memo in the case file if possible so we can turn over to the Capitol and USSS. Thanks.

Tuesday, May 27, 2014 11:34 AM

From: [redacted] USADC

To: Anzallo, Michael (MPD)

Cc: Dixon, George (MPD)

Subject: RE: Capitol case

Unfortunately, we don't release our memo. If that changes in this particular case (which would be a decision made at a much higher level than me), I will let you know. Capitol and USSS will both be doing their own reports/summaries. We won't be turning the memo over to them either. I think we will also be returning the videos to USCP, but I'm waiting for final word on that.

Tuesday, May 27, 2014 12:27 PM

From: Anzallo, Michael (MPD)

To: [redacted] USADC

Cc: Dixon, George (MPD)

Subject: RE: Capitol case

No problem [redacted.] Once we get the final decision we'll forward a copy of the file to both USSS and US Capitol. We'll also return the video to US Capitol.

The exchange explicitly mentions the risk of doing a final report (an analysis of findings of the investigation) because it might find violations of use of force policy that would make officials subject to a lawsuit. It would put Metro Police "right in the middle of the upcoming litigation," the unnamed U.S. Attorney official feared, and any opinion rendered by Internal Affairs either condemning or defending the shooting could "create a big issue."

So, Metro Police apparently never did such a report.

However, I discovered that the Justice Department did do such a report.

But the department tried to hide the existence of the report, and is still fighting to prevent its release to the public.

The e-mail chain you just read was in the material provided in response to my FOIA request by the Metro Police. However, that e-mail chain was NOT in the material provided in response to the FOIA request by the Justice Department. That demonstrates that the Justice Department was trying to hide the e-mail chain, and the existence of any discussion that the findings of an investigation would reflect poorly on federal officers and their departments.

So poorly, in fact, that the findings of an investigation would expose them to litigation.

And, the fact that the Justice Department tried to hide the existence of the e-mail chain also indicates it was trying to hide the fact that such a report exists.

But it does, in fact, exist.

Based on the responses to the FOIA requests, there had been little reason to believe such a report existed. In fact, Sanders questioned whether officials had even conducted an investigation, at all.

Sanders, with urgency in his voice, insisted to me these "smoking-gun" e-mails were evidence that there was no real investigation, only a cover-up. He also maintained that the e-mails were proof that officials did not want to issue a final report, or an analysis of whether the shooting was justified, because that might have uncovered something that could have exposed them to litigation.

The e-mails also show that both Capitol Police and the Secret Service compiled their own findings on the Carey case, with the U.S. Attorney's Office assuring the member of the MPD's internal affairs, "Capitol and USSS will both be doing their own reports/summaries."

So, where were those reports? Where were those summaries?

Why was there no final report from any agency in the FOIA material?

Where was anything that even attempted to show the deadly shooting was justified?

Nowhere to be found.

Sanders told me the e-mails showed that, not only did MPD not intend to do a final report, but the U.S. Attorney's Office may have declined to do one as well. It looked as though investigators were entirely focused on avoiding litigation, not conducting a criminal investigation or making even a cursory attempt to discover the truth.

"That's what that e-mail shows. It's telling them not to do an analysis, because they have a different department. (With different Use of Force policies.) It doesn't matter if it's a different department. They know how to read the rules," Sanders told me in an e-mail.

"If there was information that would have helped the police, they would have been all too happy to release it."

So, was an analysis even done at all?

"No, there was not," he concluded. And that seemed like a reasonable conclusion based on what was known at the time.

But then we discovered otherwise.

## 2. COVER-UP

There is plenty of evidence of a cover-up in the Carey case, but two items stand out, ironically, because they are still hidden from public view:

- a ninety-six-page DOJ memo with findings, outlining why officers did not face criminal charges for killing Carey

- surveillance videos of Carey at the White House and at the Capitol Police guard post where she was shot to death

We know the videos exist because the Justice Department released still photos from the videos of both encounters.

Why hasn't the DOJ released the videos? Sanders believes the video at the White House would show gross negligence on the part of Secret Service agents in not manning their posts and letting an unassuming Carey mistakenly drive right past them.

He also believes the videos would show that Carey did nothing to warrant agents' attempts to detain her, then chase and kill her.

But it is that ninety-six-page memo—the report with the findings of the investigation—that is the holy grail of the Carey case.

This is how we discovered the memo's existence:

There is a legal course one can take when a government agency has not fully complied with a FOIA request. One can ask for a Vaughn Index.

A Vaughn Index is a document that agencies prepare in FOIA litigation to justify information withheld under a FOIA exemption. The Judicial Watch attorney explained to me that "a defendant is not required to provide such information until they file their motion for summary judgment. However, as a courtesy and in the interest of narrowing any issues in dispute, DOJ provided us with a draft Vaughn Index."

And that's when the first eureka moment happened.

The Vaughn Index revealed that there were 140 e-mails withheld by the DOJ that looked to me very much like the findings of the investigation. They were described as "E-mail communications between the Assistant United States Attorneys who were assigned to the case and law enforcement task force that were investigating the October 3, 2013 shooting death of Miriam Carey. The documents contain the AUSA's notes, legal research, and legal theories with law enforcement officials analyzing the strength of the evidence in contemplation of litigation."

The DOJ said, in this case, that litigation referred to the potential prosecution of officers.

Then came the second eureka moment.

After I asked the Judicial Watch attorney to inquire, the

DOJ described the withheld e-mails as a "96-page declination memo," written by the U.S. attorneys assigned to the criminal investigation.

The Justice Department said: "The memo provides an overview and recommends that the US Attorney's Office for the District of Columbia decline prosecution in the police shooting death of Miriam Carey."

That is exactly what we were looking for: the key to the case. A memo containing the specific reasons why investigators concluded that the shooting and killing of Carey were justified.

But it would not be easy to get.

To justify the withholding of the memo, the DOJ cited "FOIA Exemptions b3; 18 U.S.C. § 3509(d); b5, b6 and b7C."

The legal reasons the DOJ gave for withholding the e-mails were:

"Withheld in Full (b)(5)—Attorney Work Product ((b) (6) and (b)(7)(C)—Privacy Exemption (b)(5)—attorney work product privilege is intended to protect documents and other memoranda prepared by an attorney in contemplation of litigation."

Exemption (b)(5) is the most difficult one to overcome. It is commonly used to hide anything and everything. It is a broad, umbrella exemption that allows agencies to withhold what they consider privileged inter- and intra-agency communications.

The Judicial Watch attorney told me courts tend to uniformly agree with the argument that if such material were to be exposed, it would interfere with future agency communications. And, the court traditionally has a presumption of the integrity of a federal agency.

I asked Judicial Watch to contend that the material we

sought was being withheld for reasons other than what the government was claiming.

It seemed clear to me the government was hiding information primarily because it reflected poorly on both the officers involved in the shooting and investigators.

That assertion was based on the actions the government had taken to keep as much information from the public as possible, as well as all the glaring inconsistencies I had uncovered in the official version of events, not least of which was that officers claimed to have shot an unarmed woman in the back in self-defense.

I maintained that revealing the memo would be especially in the public interest because it would show whether the shooting was justified.

The Judicial Watch lawyer indicated that those reasons appeared plausible when she said she would not be uncomfortable presenting them to the judge. The attorney did warn that the (b)(5) exemption would be a tough hurdle, but she thought we had arguments to make that could be backed up with the facts WND presented, along with the legal authority she would cite.

While writing this book, the issue was expected to take months to be resolved in court.

Another item the judge might see as evidence of a Justice Department cover-up: an odd discrepancy in the FOIA responses.

The responses from both the MPD and the DOJ to our FOIA requests contained a synopsis of the statement from the officer who pulled Carey's child out of the car, but with one major, and telling, difference.

The DOJ version redacted the last five sentences of the officer's statement.

Those particular lines describe how Carey's child was pulled from the car (after witnessing the brutal killing of her mother right in front of her face) "covered in glass and blood," and how the officer rushed to get the child treated and hospitalized.

Why would the DOJ redact those lines if not out of fear that they would show that the officers' actions were horribly incompetent and reckless?

And out of fear that the revelation would expose the Capitol Police and Secret Service to litigation because of their officers' horrendous mishandling of the incident, including the reckless endangerment and perhaps serious injury of the child?

Here is the full text of the statement:

OCTOBER 7, 2014

DET [redacted]

BRIEF SYNOPSIS OF INTERVIEW WTH USCP OFFICER [redacted]

On Thursday, October 3, 2013 this writer along with Detective [redacted] interviewed USCP Officer [redacted] at the Homicide Branch. During the interview Officer [redacted] was asked about his duties and assignment during the shooting on Capitol Hill. Officer [redacted] told this writer his assignment was Footbeat 378C. Officer [redacted] said he was standing near the intersection of First and Constitution Avenue when he observed a vehicle (hereafter referred to as Suspect vehicle) traveling towards him at a high rate of speed followed by marked police cars. Officer [redacted] said as the suspect's vehicle got closer he noticed the driver was headed directly at him. Officer [redacted] said he dove across a parked vehicle to avoid being struck by the suspect's vehicle. Officer [redacted] said the suspect's vehicle hit the car he dove across and continue [*sic*] up the crosswalk and struck the guards booth. Officer [redacted] said he rolled off the parked [car] and came up with his firearm in his hand. Officer [redacted] said he was focused on the suspect's vehicle but there were other officers in his line of fire. Officer [redacted] said the suspect attempted to back the car up toward the officers and that's when he heard multiple gunshots. Officer [redacted] said when the shots stopped he ran towards the suspect's vehicle and noticed a small child in the back seat in a car seat. Officer [redacted] said the driver was unresponsive and he signaled to the other officers there was a child in the car. Officer [redacted] said he broke the car window and pulled the child from the car. Officer [redacted] said the child was covered in glass and blood. Officer [redacted] said he wiped the child off and checked her for any injuries. Officer [redacted] said he rushed the child indoors and had a nurse treat the child. Officer [redacted] said he rode in the ambulance with the child to Children's Hospital.

These are the five sentences that were blacked out, or redacted, in the DOJ's response to the FOIA request:

Officer [redacted] said he broke the car window and pulled the child from the car. Officer [redacted] said the child was covered in glass and blood. Officer [redacted] said he wiped the child off and checked her for any injuries. Officer [redacted] said he rushed the child indoors and had a nurse treat the child. Officer [redacted] said he rode in the ambulance with the child to Children's Hospital.

Why redact those lines? There are no state secrets there.

It seems impossible to come to any conclusion other than the DOJ was trying to hide the fact that the child had been put in serious danger, narrowly escaping death.

And that she had been hospitalized.

And that she may have been seriously injured.

And why would the DOJ want to hide that information?

It could only be out of fear that it would have shown tremendous incompetence on the part of federal officers in putting a child at such risk.

The attempt to hide that information seems like clear proof of DOJ cover-up.

An attempt to bury some of the most damning facts of the case.

This small but potent example clearly indicates that the Justice Department is attempting to hide evidence in the Carey case.

There is no question that the Justice Department has stonewalled my investigation into the Carey case, refusing to turn over any significant evidence until compelled by legal action.

Is the Justice Department also conducting a cover-up?

It would seem reasonable to conclude that the feds would not be stonewalling if they did not have reason to conceal incriminating evidence.

The signs that the DOJ is stonewalling are abundant and telling. The police report was never made public until my two FOIAs forced them to do so. Why? That is not standard procedure. Former NYPD officer Sanders told me it is standard procedure to release the report once an investigation is concluded. Even though FOIA requests did at last force authorities to make the police report public, recall the list of evidence missing from the heavily redacted report: security camera videos, police radio recordings, ballistics and forensics reports, police statements, witness statements, statement transcripts. Recall that the biggest piece of missing evidence was anything at all that might demonstrate why investigators found the shooting and killing of Carey justified. No investigation analysis or findings were provided.

If investigators were so certain officers acted appropriately and that the shooting was defensible, why don't they show the public what information and reasoning they used to come to that conclusion?

All of this official silence is perhaps the biggest sign of a cover-up.

After all, what can authorities say when their official position is that they shot an unarmed woman in the back in self-defense?

What can they say when the heralded but beleaguered Secret Service chased and gunned down a woman in violation of its own policies on the use of force?

When asked why the police report did not include findings, a summary, or analysis that would justify the fatal shooting of Carey, William Miller, the public information officer for the U.S. Attorney's Office in Washington, responded: "We have no comment beyond the statement we issued last year." Interestingly, that statement—the one from U.S. Attorney Ronald Machen on July 10, 2014, exonerating the officers—itself appeared to acknowledge that the shooting death of Carey was a mistake, because it said: "Accident, mistake, fear, negligence and bad judgment do not establish such a criminal violation."

When asked about that later, Miller replied in an e-mail, "No such acknowledgment was made in that statement. That language can typically be found in press releases involving such investigations. It refers to the law as a general matter, not the specific case."

But then, why not make public, for all eyes to see, the findings that the shooting was justified?

## 3. HISTORY REPEATS

The stonewall and apparent cover-up began under Attorney General Eric Holder and continued under Loretta Lynch, who succeeded him on April 27, 2015.

For all of the Obama administration's publicly declared outrage over the killing of other unarmed black victims by police, Holder's record shows surprising indifference to such shootings.

In fact, the Carey case may fit a pattern, exhibiting parallels with other police shootings under Holder when he was U.S. attorney for the District of Columbia.

Another little-known police shooting in the nation's capital may be illustrative. In that case, an officer shot an unarmed suspect in the back four times while he was lying on the ground. The shooter was never even interviewed by police. The man in charge of that investigation?

Eric Holder.

Police shootings in Washington were the subject of a Pulitzer Prize–winning *Washington Post* investigation in 1998. The five-part series indicated that Holder's performance as an investigator of police shootings was dismal.[1]

As U.S. Attorney for the District of Columbia from 1993 to 1997, Holder was in charge of investigating police shootings by local officers. The *Post* investigation discovered that the number of people shot by Washington police doubled between 1988 and 1995. Sixteen people were shot by police under Holder's watch in 1995 alone.[2] Worse, not only did police shootings mushroom during his tenure, but almost one-third of those between 1994 and 1997 weren't even counted by his department.[3]

The paper published a map showing that from 1994 to 1998 Washington police shot twenty civilians. Eight of them died.

*USA Today* revived the *Post* investigation in the wake of the Ferguson shooting with an opinion piece by author James Bovard, who declared that during Holder's reign he did "little to protect Washington residents from rampaging lawmen" as police violence "spiraled out of control."

The article went on to say that Holder largely ignored abusive actions by police as civilians were shot and killed by officers at a rate higher than any other major city police department. Bovard concluded that Holder's promise to conduct a full and fair investigation of the shooting in Ferguson was belied by his "own record." In fact, during Holder's tenure, assistant Washington police chief Terrance Gainer even had to admit, "We shoot too often, and we shoot too much when we do shoot."[4]

The *Post* found Washington police were not prosecuted by Holder even when police review boards ruled that shootings were unjustified or they discovered contradictions in officers' testimony.[5]

The solution? Kill the review board.

Even after a judge blasted the Washington government

for "deliberate indifference" to charges of police brutality, the Civilian Complaint Review Board, overwhelmed by a glut of complaints, was shut down in 1995.[6]

Bovard said the *Post* series caused such an uproar that it sparked a Justice Department Civil Rights Division investigation into five years of Washington police shootings, but "who did Attorney General Janet Reno put in charge of that effort? Eric Holder."[7]

Holder's office denied any conflict of interest, but Michael Morgenstern, the attorney for a couple who successfully sued the district for $150,000 after an officer shot and killed their son in 1995, told the *Post*, "When I heard who was conducting the review, I could just feel my blood boiling because you've got the hen guarding the foxes."[8]

Morgenstern scornfully said of Holder, "He had the opportunity to do this when he was there, and now all of a sudden, they're sending him back to do the same job he didn't do while he was there."[9]

Here's how some of the information the *Post* uncovered has been echoed in the Carey case: According to the paper, a number of officer shootings of civilians under Holder's watch were kept from the public view, with police investigating in secret and producing reports only when ordered to by a judge.[10] Similarly, the police report in the Carey case was never released until the mayor's office ordered MPD to comply with a FOIA request, and the DOJ never complied until it was taken to court.

Also similarly, the findings in the Carey shooting were never released. The public was merely told there was insufficient evidence to bring charges, but was never allowed to see the evidence or the report.

The *Post* also found that some of the worst cases of police abuse under Holder involved officers shooting into cars, which is strongly discouraged due to the risk of hitting bystanders. Holder said he did not recall more than a few such instances, but the *Post* discovered more than fifty officers had shot at unarmed drivers over five years.[11]

The paper also reported instances of police perjury in some of those shootings. And, the *Post* learned Washington police shot at cars twenty times more often than New York City police.[12]

Officers shot at Carey's car twenty-six times.

Statistics on officer shootings are hard to come by because most police departments do not publish those numbers, and the federal government doesn't either, despite the fact that in 1994 Congress ordered the attorney general to publish an annual summary on the use of excessive force by police officers as part of the Violent Crime and Law Enforcement Control Act.

Even government statisticians have had to use Google News alerts to track officer-involved shootings.

There is one source researchers often use: former FBI agent Jim Fisher methodically combed the Internet to compile the number of police shootings in 2011.[13]

From the information that can be gleaned, police shootings in the nation's capital did not appear to have gotten much better under Holder as attorney general, where he was the top law enforcement official in the district, as well as the nation.

Fisher's website did not list police shootings in the nation's capital, but he told me in an e-mail that there were eleven in Washington, D.C., in 2011, six of which were fatal.

An Internet search showed at least four police shootings in

the nation's capital in 2012 and another four in 2013.

All of those numbers appear to dwarf officer-involved shootings by St. Louis County police in the Ferguson, Missouri, area. As far as can be discerned by an Internet search, the last police shooting of civilians by the department was in Berkeley, a town adjacent to Ferguson, in 2000. Two unarmed men were shot as part of a drug bust. Two officers involved said they feared for their lives, the shootings were ruled justified, and they were not indicted.

So, why did Holder pay such attention to the Michael Brown shooting? He said he hoped his visit would help calm the area. But the attorney general specifically cited race as a reason for going to Ferguson. He told residents there, "I am the Attorney General of the United States. But I am also a black man."[14]

The nation's top law enforcement official recounted the humiliation and anger he felt in earlier years after being stopped for speeding twice on the New Jersey turnpike, and the "impact" it had on him. Holder referred to the racial "mistrust and mutual suspicion" between the black community and law enforcement.[15]

But race did not appear to motivate Holder to crack down on the epidemic of police shootings in Washington, D.C., either during his tenure as U.S. attorney or as attorney general. That was despite the fact, after his selection by President Clinton in 1993, Holder was the first African-American to become the district's U.S. attorney.

Despite the dearth of data, it would stand to reason that a significant number of police shooting victims during Holder's time as U.S. attorney were black, as African-Americans comprise

Washington's largest ethnic group, at more than 50 percent of the population. But instead of making any apparent attempt to ease tensions between the black community and police, his department became the subject of a Justice Department investigation into police abuse.

So why did Holder personally become involved in the Ferguson case and launch a federal investigation of that shooting yet virtually ignore the Carey killing in his own backyard?

The key difference seems to be it was his own officers who killed Carey.

## 4. THE WHISTLE-BLOWER

Proof of a cover-up arrived in the mail just before this book went to press, when a whistle-blower blew the lid off the Carey case with a series of bombshell revelations.

An anonymous Capitol Police officer, writing on behalf of fellow officers, bluntly stated that the department had murdered Carey.

The whistle-blower accused the department of covering up the crime and provided tangible evidence of police misconduct in the form of secret department documents.

Copies of the Capitol Police policies on the use of force and vehicular pursuits showed that police had violated their own rules in chasing and gunning down Carey.

The whistle-blower said the department was terrified of the case.

The letters were sent to Eric Sanders, who told me the author was definitely a Capitol Police officer who knew "inside details only an employee would know."

Sanders said he received one letter in February 2015 and a

follow-up letter in March 2016. The most recent letter revealed the following:

- Capitol Police officers believe Carey was murdered.

- Superiors forced officers on the scene to change their statements.

- Officers had never seen an investigation handled in that fashion.

- Officers expected the government to stonewall inquiries into the case.

- The Capitol Police chief and assistant chief were so uncomfortable with the case that the former considered resigning and the latter actually did.

The letter substantiated much of my reporting and contradicted much of the official version of events, including the contention that there was insufficient evidence to bring criminal charges against officers for Carey's death.

The Capitol Police officer who penned the letter did not merely make a claim that Carey was murdered; instead, the officer stated it as a fact, writing:

I doubt members of Congress would have cheered on the House floor when Ms. Carey was murdered........which was obscene and pathetic.

The whistle-blower described how officers were made to change their stories:

Officers on the scene the day Ms. Carey died had to give written statements, but they were brought in to watch the video of the shooting so they could amend their statement to go along with the video.

That's because the police knew they were in the wrong:

This was obviously done in case the Justice Department decided to prosecute and to build up the Department's defense if you ever get this case to court.

Officers found the investigation fishy:

I have never heard of investigations being handled in this fashion. I had heard a couple officers complaining about this. I don't have their phone numbers, but their names are [redacted] and [redacted.][16]

The whistle-blower and fellow officers saw a cover-up:

What we don't understand is how the Justice Department will do a complete analysis of the police departments in Ferguson and Baltimore, but ignores your simple request for transparency in Ms. Carey's case.

The officer did not believe justice was done, and encouraged Sanders to pursue the truth despite the cover-up:

I was so happy to learn that you did file the lawsuit. While I fully expect the government to stonewall you, please don't give up.

One of the reasons not to give up was that even Capitol Police leadership was extremely uncomfortable with the case:

There are rumors that the Carey case was one of the reasons the chief [Kim Dine] wanted to resign, instead assistant chief [Daniel] Malloy retired. Many people believe it is because he is African American and he had problems with the entire incident, which would make sense since his wife has had a long standing lawsuit against the capitol police for harassment and discrimination.

The whistle-blower again made it clear that Carey was unjustly killed when he pleaded:

Please help the Carey family get the justice they deserve.

To top it all off, the anonymous officer made the stunning revelation that most Capitol Police officers also appear to believe Carey was unjustly killed:

I hope some of this helps you, please start reaching out to those of us that work for the Capitol Police, I'm sure the majority of employees would be forthcoming.

The whistle-blower also provided damning, tangible evidence that confirmed that the killing of Miriam Carey was unjustified: copies of the Capitol Police Department's Use of Force and Vehicular Pursuit policies.

Although kept secret from the public, the policies are not classified, but labeled merely "law enforcement sensitive." Even so, WND did not publish the documents, only the information contained within them that was relevant to the Carey case.

It appears that was the first time information in those policies has been made public.

The documents make it clear that Capitol Police officers

violated their own policies on the use of force and vehicle pursuits when they chased, shot, and killed Carey.

Here is what the documents reveal:

- Officers are permitted to use deadly force only when a life is threatened or in danger of serious injury.

- It is not permissible to use deadly force merely to keep a suspect from escaping.

- Police may conduct a vehicle chase only of a violent felon, or someone suspected of committing a violent felony.

- Officers must decide whether the danger to the public is more important than capturing the suspect.

Those points all indicate Capitol Police made a grave mistake in chasing and killing Carey, according to their own policies.

Perhaps the most revealing fact: neither the Capitol Police Use of Force guidelines nor the Vehicular Pursuit policy says a vehicle can be considered a deadly weapon (which is also true of the policies of most major metropolitan police departments, including the Washington, D.C., Metropolitan Police).

That is relevant because officers claimed they shot and killed Carey in self-defense.

But Carey was unarmed. So if her car was not a weapon, then the officers' lives couldn't have been considered endangered, by the Capitol Police Department's own legal standards.

Capitol Police policy on the use of force does allow officers to use deadly force if they feel their own lives are in danger:

An officer may use deadly force only when the officer reasonably believes that the action is in defense of human life, including the officer's own life, or in the defense of any person in immediate danger of serious physical injury.

And according to the police report, that is the claim made by the first officer who fired at Carey—to reiterate a point made earlier in this book with new urgency—that "in fear for his life," he "discharged his service pistol several times at the suspect's vehicle as she fled the scene."

"As she fled the scene." Now, that's illuminating language.

Who finds himself in danger of someone who is "fleeing" from him? Picture someone who is running away from you, or fleeing, as it were. Would you be "in fear" for your life?

There's also documentation showing that officers' lives were not endangered at the second shooting scene in evidence provided by the Justice Department itself, in the form of photographs. Take another look at the sequence of photos in the section titled "Witnesses versus Officers" near the end of chapter 2. You will see that the photos clearly show the officers did not appear to be in danger.

But, still, they shot and killed Carey.

The Capitol Police policy on use of force even makes a special point of making officers aware that they must not shoot if the suspect poses no threat:

NOTE: The U.S. Supreme Court decision in Tennessee v. Garner states that the use of deadly force to prevent the escape of all felony suspects, whatever the circumstances, is constitutionally unreasonable. Officers cannot shoot a fleeing felon who poses no threat to the safety of the officer(s) or others.

The policy also declares:

> Discharging a firearm at or from a moving vehicle will be governed by this use of force policy and is prohibited if it presents an unreasonable risk to the officer(s) or others.

Based on material obtained by FOIA requests, there is ample evidence that officers put many members of the public in grave danger, particularly by shooting at Carey's car in Garfield Circle. As noted earlier in this book, according to the police report, thirty bystanders were in Garfield Circle when police fired, compelled to scramble and duck for cover as shots rang out. And potentially hundreds of people were also within range of the gunshots at tourist sites, on adjacent streets, and in nearby buildings.

The Capitol Police's General Policy on Vehicular Pursuits is very clear regarding when officers may chase a suspect, and under what conditions:

> When operating an authorized USCP pursuit vehicle with emergency devices activated, sworn employees may engage in pursuit of a vehicle only to effect the arrest or prevent the escape of a person who has committed a violent felony, has attempted to commit a violent felony in the employee's presence, or a violent felony has been committed and the employee has probable cause to believe the person he/she is attempting to apprehend has committed the felony. The felony must involve an actual or threatened attack which the employee has probable cause to believe could result in death or serious bodily injury.

But, as also noted previously, Carey was never accused of committing even a petty crime, much less a violent felony.

The Capitol Police policy guidelines on whether to continue a pursuit state:

> The object of any police pursuit is to apprehend a law violator without causing unnecessary peril to the suspects and employees involved, or to the persons or property of bystanders. With that in mind, when determining whether a pursuit should be initiated or continued, the sworn employee must balance the danger to the public by allowing the suspect to escape with the danger to the public by continuing the pursuit.

All of which begs the question: Why didn't they just let her go?

What threat outweighed the danger to the public? It appears there *was* no such threat, and that is what the Justice Department was trying to cover up, along with the shooting of an unarmed woman that hardly appears justified, when it decided not to file any criminal charges against the officers who killed—or as the whistle-blower put it, "murdered"—Carey.

Another bombshell from the whistle-blower: Capitol Police Department superiors are "terrified" of the Carey case.

In another explosive letter, this one written a year before the letter cited earlier, the same Capitol Hill Police officer:

- implied that there was a government cover-up in the Carey case

- suggested that "neglect" by officers in the Carey case contributed to a death that could have been prevented

- stated that officers should have faced criminal charges for killing Carey, but the Justice Department "failed" to make them do so

- described the department's fear of the public's reaction if the truth of the Carey case were ever to be revealed

At the time, the whistle-blower wrote:

The most recent event involving the Capitol Police during the president's State of the Union address has also brought Ms. Carey's issue to light. The fact that members of Congress want to know how an armed-robbery suspect was let go by the Capitol Police while Ms. Carey ended up dead should also help in your cause.

The whistle-blower was referring to a strikingly similar incident during President Obama's State of the Union address on January 20, 2015, that had a strikingly different outcome.

- During the speech, officers engaged in a high-speed chase of a robbery suspect in a White Ford Crown Victoria.

- The suspect reportedly ran seven red lights at speeds up to 80 miles per hour.

- The suspect nearly struck Capitol Police and Supreme Court officers.

- The suspect was only stopped by a snowplow near the Rayburn House Office Building.

- The suspect resisted arrest by refusing to leave his car until an officer tackled him to the ground.

- The suspect did not even have a driver's license.

- Capitol Police officers released the suspect without even arresting him.

That caused the whistle-blower to remark:

> There have been rumors the Department is terrified of the two cases being brought up simultaneously because it will revive interest and talk about Ms. Carey. Whether you have to force Congress, go through the media, or demonstrate on Capitol Hill, I do hope you continue to fight on behalf of the Carey family, especially for the child she left behind.

At the time, Capitol Police public relations officer Lt. Kimberly Schneider claimed the suspect in the 2015 incident did not pose a threat to the Capitol, and said in a statement, "Particularly on State of the Union night when the USCP's primary mission to protect the Congress with an operationally enhanced, hardened perimeter is our primary focus."[17]

However, protecting Congress and the White House were reasons the police gave for chasing and killing Miriam Carey.

And, the difference in the outcomes of the State of the Union incident and the Carey chase could not have been more stark. One person walked away; the other was carried away—dead.

After the State of the Union incident, I sent a series of questions about both chases to Lieutenant Schneider:

- How do you account for the obvious difference in the way this chase ended, with the suspect not arrested and let go, and the deadly way the chase of Miriam Carey ended on October 3, 2013?

- Why was it necessary to shoot her but not him?

- Why did you say this man did not pose a threat to Capitol security when the Carey chase was portrayed as such?

- Why were responding officers ordered to release the suspect by Capitol Police superiors?

- Why was this suspect not even arrested, as Jim Konczos, chairman of the Capitol Police Labor Committee's executive board, said he should have been?

Lieutenant Schneider did not respond.

Sanders says he knows why.

"What it boils down to is that they decided to not make the same critical tactical and legal mistakes they made in the Miriam Carey case."

He added, "Frankly, they know the same rules of engagement applied in the Miriam Carey case except, in her case, they lost complete supervisory control over their personnel."

That sentiment seemed to be shared by rank-and-file Capitol Hill Police officers, on whose behalf the whistle-blower wrote:

> The fact that members of Congress want to know how an armed robbery suspect was let go by the Capitol Police while Ms. Carey ended up dead should also help in your cause.

And that was exactly what happened. Elected representatives noticed the discrepancies in the outcome of the cases, and the State of the Union incident sparked renewed interest in the Carey case.

Rep. Mark Amodei (R-NV) said he wanted to look into Capitol Police protocols for traffic crimes and, in reference to

Carey, noted, "The other thing that pops into my mind is what made this different than the young lady who got shot up here last year."[18]

A former prosecutor who served as an Army Judge Advocate General Corps officer and assistant U.S. attorney, Amodei also noted that Carey committed "a series of some pretty serious traffic offenses, but nothing else that we know of . . . So anyhow, that's something we'll look into."

Amodei serves on the House Appropriations subcommittee that sets the Capitol Police's budget.

Rep. Debbie Wasserman Schultz (D-FL) is the ranking member of that subcommittee and told reporters she would discuss the incident with Capitol Police chief Kim C. Dine.[19]

Senate Rules and Administration chairman Roy Blunt (R-MO) also said he wanted to dig deeper.

However, when I sent e-mails to those lawmakers, and more than one hundred others, asking if they would call for a congressional investigation into the Carey shooting, there was not one response.

The anonymous Capitol Police officer serving as whistle-blower apparently did so at some risk to his or her job, as the initial letter boldly asserted that officers should have been criminally charged in the death of Carey:

> Sir, I am writing this in confidence since my job with the United States Capitol Police would be in jeopardy for pub-licly coming forward. First, please give my condolences to the family of Ms. Miriam Carey for their loss. While the U.S. attorney has failed to prosecute the officers involved in the actual shooting, I would like you to focus on another aspect

of this tragedy, one that was vaguely mentioned in the article, the neglect of the Capitol Police.

That "neglect" concerned what the whistle-blower claimed was a misuse by Capitol Police of the huge, metal "pop-up" barriers that officers can trigger to rise in the middle of Washington streets to stop traffic, and were installed after the terror attacks of September 11, 2001.

> It is well known throughout the Department that the Capitol Police were operating the "pop-up" barriers on the Avenues without procedures in place. This is especially relevant since when Ms. Carey was driving towards Capitol Hill, the officers operating the safety barriers would have/should have raised these barriers, and this alone would have prevented Ms. Carey from driving up Constitution Avenue where she was ultimately shot.

The whistle-blower buttressed the assertion that the barriers had been dangerously operated by including a copy of an article in *Roll Call* about a horrible accident involving the barriers about a half year before the Carey incident.

According to the article, on February 13, 2013, a motorcycle officer "sped off to stop a car that had run a red light just as one of the barriers was coming up and he was severely injured."

The article continued, "Certain changes to protocol at security checkpoints should have been addressed seven months ago, said Capitol Police Labor Committee President Jim Konczos, when he and his colleagues reached out to Tom Reynolds, then the acting Capitol Police chief, to express their concerns."

The whistle-blower felt that proper use of the barriers could have saved Carey's life, and, instead, improper use nearly killed an officer:

> While people may speculate as to the outcome, there was a high probability Ms. Carey's vehicle would have been diverted with the proper use of the barricades making the outcome of this much different. The fact that the Capitol Police almost killed one of their own shows the uncertainty in which many of these officers routinely operate. There has even been talk that the officers working these avenues did not have up-to-date training to operate these barriers, which shows negligence on the [part of] Capitol Police.

The officer who was almost killed, referred to in this letter, was in a Capitol Police cruiser chasing Carey that slammed into a security barrier when it suddenly popped up on Constitution Avenue. The car struck the barrier with such force that witnesses thought they'd heard an explosion. The collision caused an injury to an officer requiring an airlift to the hospital. The officer recovered, but the chase was not immediately halted, even after that near tragedy.

As previously noted, it is a violation of the Capitol Police vehicular pursuit policy to continue a pursuit when an officer's or civilian's life has been put in danger.

## 5. HARASSMENT

Sanders believes he was harassed and targeted by the feds because of his dogged pursuit of justice for Carey.

The attorney has faced a number of obstacles while representing Carey's family, but none as challenging as one that happened behind the scenes: a government threat to disbar him.

That civil contempt investigation was suddenly and mysteriously dropped in March 2015, as suddenly and mysteriously
as it began.

Sanders was arrested at his Long Island, New York, home
on October 15, 2013, just one day after he held a press conference in Brooklyn and called on the Justice Department to
investigate the Carey death, while also warning, "You cannot
trust the government."

Sanders said the judge who brought the civil contempt
charge against him, U.S. bankruptcy judge Dorothy Eisenberg,
suddenly retired without explanation at the same time the
charge was dropped.

And, just as mysteriously, the official transcript of the case
that led to the charges simply disappeared without explanation.

Sanders said he had tried to obtain that transcript from four
different courts without success.

When I asked back on December 3, 2013, if he felt his arrest
was an attempt to either silence or intimidate him, the attorney
laughed loud and long.

"Of course I think it was! I can't prove it," he said. "I loved
the timing of it—the day after our press conference. Exactly one
day after I said don't trust the government."

Sanders insisted he had no debts and declared a bankruptcy
solely to fight a judgment and to protect his client. He was
still fighting the judgment in which he was ordered to make
back payments to a coworker because, he said, the court erred
in finding that he was her employer. Sanders said he was a
fellow employee, and it was their former boss who owed her
the judgment.

"I am clean. That's the way I was as a cop. That's the way I am as an attorney," he told me. "I was a police officer in New York. I've never been arrested in my life. The question is, why was I picked up?"

After his arrest, Sanders spent a nightmarish six days in a federal prison with murder suspects and other accused felons.

He said the court refused to see him for close to a week, traumatizing him, jeopardizing his safety, and harming his "squeaky-clean image as an African-American legal professional," while also negatively affecting his family, friends, and clients.

The New York–based attorney said the unjust incarceration cost him millions of dollars in business, as well as damage to his prestige.

And, after all that damage was done, the government simply dropped the case.

Sanders provided a copy of a document from the U.S. District Court, Eastern District of New York, dated March 20, 2015, that simply read:

> The Committee on Grievances of the Eastern District of New York, having reviewed the relevant documents in 13-MC-885, has determined that no action is warranted.

It was signed by Paula Marie Susi, case manager/attorney disciplinary clerk.

"Isn't that interesting?" Sanders mused rhetorically about the lack of any explanation as to either why the charge was brought or dropped.

Once his name was cleared, he began fighting back.

Sanders issued a statement declaring:

Retired bankruptcy Judge Dorothy T. Eisenberg and the attorneys involved in these matters intentionally, in a mean-spirited vindictive manner, damaged my stellar personal and business reputation affecting the handling of this and other client legal matters. Their collective actions caused "irreparable damage" to me and lost revenue to The Sanders Firm, P.C.

Therefore, in the very near future, I will be filing complaints with the Second Circuit and related Bar Associations about the conduct of retired bankruptcy Judge Dorothy T. Eisenberg and the attorneys, then file a series of federal torts claims and lawsuits related to violations of my civil rights along with related state and common law legal claims.

## 6. MURDER

More than a year before the discovery of all the damning evidence revealed in the FOIA documents, a number of distinguished legal experts had already concluded the killing of Miriam Carey was not justified.

The American Civil Liberties Union shied away from weighing in on the killing, sending me a statement that read, "Unfortunately, we don't have anyone available to comment on this incident."

But four leading experts in civil liberties and law enforcement who agreed to comment for the record concluded the incident should have been handled differently and that Carey should not be dead.

- Nat Hentoff is one of the nation's top authorities on civil liberties and the First Amendment. He was a columnist and staff writer with the *Village Voice* for fifty-one years, from

1957 until 2008, when he became a weekly columnist for WND. Hentoff was a Pulitzer Prize finalist in 1999 for his weekly columns championing free expression and individual rights. He is a senior fellow at the CATO Institute.

- John W. Whitehead is an attorney, author, and expert on constitutional law and human rights. He has filed numerous amicus briefs before the U.S. Supreme Court and been co-counsel in several landmark Supreme Court cases. He is the president of the Rutherford Institute, a nonprofit civil liberties and human rights organization he founded. Articles by Whitehead have been printed in the *New York Times*, *Los Angeles Times*, *Washington Post*, and *USA Today*. His most recent book is *A Government of Wolves: The Emerging American Police State* (New York: SelectBooks, 2013).

- Dan Bongino was a Secret Service agent for twelve years, guarding presidents Bill Clinton, George W. Bush, and Barack Obama. He is the author of the *New York Times* best seller *Life Inside the Bubble: Why a Top-Ranked Secret Service Agent Walked Away from It All*, published by WND Books.

- Richard Mack, former sheriff of Graham County, Arizona, spent twenty years in law enforcement and the past seventeen years as an activist and crusader for freedom. He has appeared at more than 120 Tea Party rallies all across America and has authored five books regarding states' rights, the oath of office, and constitutional liberty. He won a landmark Supreme Court decision on the issue of states' rights and local independence after filing a lawsuit against the Clinton administration to stop the gun control associated with the Brady Bill.

Hentoff, a former board member of the American Civil Liberties Union, said he believes police murdered the unarmed young mother. In a lengthy phone call, he told me, based on all the evidence he had seen in WND's reports (which he called "very thorough" and "easily corroborated"), "This is a classic case of police out of control and, therefore, guilty of plain murder."

Hentoff said it is an exceedingly important story because the case could have ominous implications for the entire country.

Someone must be held accountable for Carey's death, Hentoff maintained. Otherwise, it could set what he called a very damaging precedent.

"The evidence pointing against them, that they killed recklessly, is so strong that if there is not a thorough investigation by someone other than the police . . ."

Hentoff let the thought hang in the air, then added, "The problem is, I don't trust the FBI anymore, or any of our other intelligence agencies."

Hentoff wasn't alone among legal scholars in his assessment that police were lethally out of control on that day in early October 2013.

Whitehead reviewed the evidence and I asked him in an e-mail if he thought Carey was murdered.

"In my opinion, yes," he answered. "I think it was what they call a 'bad shot,' yes."

Former Graham County, Arizona, sheriff Richard Mack concluded, "Miriam Carey should have been arrested, not shot." He called the handling of Carey "sloppy" police work and saw "no justification whatsoever" for the use of deadly force against her.

Based on his experience in similar situations, Bongino told me during a phone call he understood the actions of law enforcement officers in a fast-moving and confusing situation and was loath to evaluate their decisions in hindsight. But as a former Secret Service agent, he felt the situation at the White House could have been handled better and doubted that those involved, or their superiors, would dispute that.

Admitting that the incident was absolutely not handled effectively, Bongino predicted it would lead to changes, including retraining and security modifications.

Bongino believes the problem actually originated almost two hundred years ago because the south entrance to the White House, although secure, was designed in the early 1800s.

He thought there would be "a serious remodel" of some of the security on the south side of the White House following the incident. The former protector of the president didn't want to divulge too much about security measures there, but he did say there appeared to be an access-control issue.

"She turned into a little pocket there, and anybody can turn in there," he said. "She got caught up and sped off. You wouldn't be able to do that at another secure government building. They use vehicle traps."

Bongino had tremendous empathy for his former colleagues in the Secret Service and declined to second-guess their split-second decisions in a confusing situation.

Noting the unique nature of the White House, he pointed out how agents working up to twenty-hour days are surrounded by threats. The White House is a big target, he explained. The president is an even bigger target.

"When the president's in the White House, it's even worse," he said. "You're constantly on edge."

Still, Bongino conceded that the authorities may have overreacted.

"The libertarian in me thinks this was a very dangerous incident for civil liberties," he said. "The fact you could have, perhaps, a condition and an extremely bad day and wind up dead, of course, should bother all of us."

"What happened to this woman is an extraordinary example of how police have no limits when they get into this sort of situation," maintained Hentoff.

Mack and Whitehead both strongly believed the police should have handled the car chase much differently and that they ignored a number of nonlethal alternatives, such as disabling her car with tire spikes.

I asked Whitehead if the actions of the police have been warranted because of so-called high-value targets at the Capitol and the White House.

"No," he answered, adding that he believes police overreacted by shooting at Carey when they could have employed an alternative.

"Why didn't they just shoot her tires out?" he wondered. "Or why not use nonlethal weapons? They're stacked with them. Stop the car. She's a female with a kid in the car. If it turns out she's crazy, you can take her down with a Taser. Or pepper spray. Do it properly."

Mack provided an analysis of the evidence in an e-mail, identifying a key missed opportunity when police first had Carey's car surrounded, which was precisely when they should have blocked her in with their vehicles.

Indeed, the video shot by a news crew at Garfield Circle shows police had that opportunity. Instead, two, perhaps even three, cruisers parked behind Carey's car, rather than boxing her in on the passenger side. They also failed to block the front of her car.

Because officers did not surround Carey then and there, they left her a clear path to leave the scene. The audio on the video recorded police firing at least seven shots as she departed.

The former sheriff said firing those shots under those circumstances is against policy in most police agencies, but, "regardless, Carey's action did not even come close to allowing police shooting at her."

The fact that there was a child in the car further complicated the decision to shoot, and based on the previously described evidence, officers should have known of the child's presence.

Also, the video shows five of the six officers who surrounded her vehicle on foot appeared to get an extremely close and clear look inside the car. It would seem difficult to believe that at least one of them did not see the toddler in the car seat.

Mack said they had to have seen that a child was in the car, making the need for restraint by the police even more necessary. Furthermore, he said the use of deadly force under those circumstances should have been absolutely forbidden.

"The police showed utter indifference for the safety of the baby and fired their guns without provocation," he concluded. "The decedent [Carey] did violate some traffic laws, but such does not give police justification for using lethal force."

Hentoff and Whitehead both firmly believe the case was an example of a growing "shoot first, ask questions later" mentality spreading across the nation among law enforcement agencies. They argue it is directly related to a change in training and a militarization of police departments across the country.

Whitehead said the danger the officers created to public safety reminded him of a September 14, 2013, incident when New York police officers fired three shots on a crowded

Manhattan street near Times Square, missing the man they mistakenly believed had a weapon but hitting two bystanders.

(And that followed another one in August 2012, when New York police fired sixteen shots and hit nine bystanders, outside one of the world's most popular tourist attractions, the Empire State Building, as a large crowd watched.)

Whitehead said the "shoot first, ask questions later" problem begins at police academies. A chief of police who teaches at academies informed him that rookies are learning a militarized version of law enforcement.

"They shoot when told to," said the attorney. "They're not acting like peace officers anymore. They're not questioning authority at all. They operate like an army. There's a mentality now that they're the bosses because they have the guns."

According to Whitehead, a range of psychological factors condition officers to act more like soldiers, from the militarized, black uniforms to the ubiquitous use of SWAT teams. "All the federal agencies have SWAT teams now," said Whitehead. "As I show in my book, the Department of Education has SWAT teams. There have been SWAT team raids on people for overdue loans."

He said his book also documents all the "crazy examples of the strip searches and rectal exams on the streets."

Whitehead said he works with many police officers who tell him it has become a problem, but they don't know what to do. One even told him he dropped out of the police academy because of what he called "the thug complex" they're teaching police.

"They're so 'code blue' . . . 'We're a gang, we move together, and if something happens we don't rat on each other.'"

He believes the militarization of the police began in the 1980s, when the Department of Defense "began handing out all this equipment," such as MRAPs, or Mine Resistant Ambush Protected vehicles.

When asked if the equipment was introduced to fight rising crime, Whitehead instead saw a profit motive by the corporations that make the tank-like vehicles and have made a lot of money by lobbying the government.

Whitehead said there's a sinister alliance between federal and local authorities that results in suppressed dissent and violations of basic First Amendment rights. "There's a mentality now that's led to Homeland Security raiding veterans' homes for anti-Obama rants, those kinds of crazy things," he told me over the phone. "They're working with the local police. They work in teams now."

Whitehead told me the militarization of local police slowed under former President George W. Bush but picked up speed under Obama. "It's a standing army now," he reflected. "I am surprised sometimes, how local police approach citizens. Very authoritative, for minor offenses."

Whitehead indicated he believes Homeland Security is actually turning into a national police force. "We don't even have local police in the true sense anymore," he insisted. "They're extensions of the federal government."

That's because most Americans don't understand that the Fourth Amendment of the Constitution prevents police from such outrageous practices as strip searches without probable cause, he argued. "The average American, if you mention the Fourth Amendment, a huge question mark forms in their brain. Then they go watch TV."

Hentoff agrees that "there is no question" about the growing militarization of the police. He found the Carey case a particularly ominous harbinger, indicating that the country is in "severe danger" of becoming a police state. The nation is not there yet, he said, because the First Amendment is still working, and independent media are still free to sound the alarm.

But, contends the civil libertarian, the Carey case dramatized some serious underlying tendencies toward becoming a police state, judging by reports he has heard from around the country. He believes the only thing that could put a limit on police power would be accountability.

"Because the evidence is so strong that the police recklessly killed Miriam Carey," Hentoff said, "the officers involved and their superiors must be held to account for her death, for the sake of the country."

Hentoff worries that if stories such as this were allowed to die, the danger of becoming a true police state would only increase. That is why he believes it to be such a critical story. "Because, if we are ever going to become a police state," he says, "eventually the First Amendment will die along with this poor woman."

The highly acclaimed journalist commended WND for pursuing the story, saying that it is important because, if police can get away with murder, "What kind of country are we?"

## 7. JUSTICE

Justice may yet come for Miriam Carey.

The Carey family still wants criminal charges filed against the officers who killed her.

But, they may have to settle for a financial penalty against the government.

If the family files a civil suit and a jury finds in their favor, it would at least be a public admission that officers wrongly killed Carey.

More likely, the government would do anything to settle the case before it went to a jury, because, if the Justice Department had already spent years stonewalling the facts from reaching the public, it would doubtless spend as much of the people's money as it would take to keep the lid on the case.

The family has taken the first steps toward filing a lawsuit against those responsible for the killing of Carey.

Carey family attorney Eric Sanders filed a $200 million conspiracy claim in April 2015 against the Department of Justice, the U.S. Secret Service, and the U.S. Capitol. A wrongful death claim of $150 million for "numerous intentional, grossly negligent and reckless actions of police officers, supervisors, managers and other related employees" previously had been denied.

The claim maintained that Carey had not violated any law, and, therefore, police had "no legal basis to stop her or use any amount of physical force against her."

Sanders asserted it was officers who endangered Carey's safety, not the other way around. He said the ensuing car chase also endangered the public, outweighing "the benefit of investigating a harmless mistaken entrance through the White House entrance gate."

These federal tort claims are the first legal steps toward filing a pair of lawsuits, totaling $350 million, against the defendants for the shooting death of Carey.

Sanders said the conspiracy claim is that authorities are trying to cover up the wrongful death of Carey. The additional claim was necessary because authorities were "actively blocking" attempts to gain the information needed to file a successful lawsuit, and were "covering up details."

"They denied the first claim but gave no information why," he told me.

The second claim, he explained, will also help to keep the statute of limitations from expiring. Technically, he said, there is no time limit in constitutional cases, but in practice, there is generally a three- to four-year window.

The second claim seeks:

- $50 million for the estate of Miriam Carey;

- $50 million for her mother, Idella Carey;

- $50 million for Miriam's infant daughter; and

- $50 million for Miriam's sister, Valarie.

The Carey family has long put the pursuit of justice for Miriam above any financial gain. More than once, the family has insisted it is much more interested in justice than in filing lawsuits.

But, Sanders believes a lawsuit may be what it takes to get the government to reveal what really happened to Miriam, and how a simple trip from her home in Stamford, Connecticut, to the nation's capital ended up costing the thirty-four-year-old her life.

"You will never, ever hear them discuss the Miriam Carey case unless the courts allow the case to move forward," insisted Sanders.

The attorney said the suit would be to compensate the family for their "great loss of a daughter, mother, friend, and confidant." But he asserts the case is about more than the death of just one woman. He says it represents a threat to the rights of all Americans.

"Somehow, the Bill of Rights did not apply to Miriam. Miriam's life did not seem to be so important. Thus far, Miriam's death is being treated as simple collateral damage in the government's zeal to protect itself from terrorism."

That zeal should not eclipse the importance of human life, he contends.

"The framers of the United States Constitution fought for, died for, and demanded it. We should expect no different in today's society, either."

Sanders told me that, at the very least, authorities should have taken what they have learned from the Carey case on car stops, vehicle pursuits, and the use of force and announced policy changes to the public. "These public disclosures are absolutely necessary because Miriam's death unfolded right before the international community via live television."

Sanders wrote to then attorney general Eric Holder to request a civil rights investigation but never received a response.

Miriam's sister, Valarie, called for a congressional investigation.

"The United States Congress using its legislative powers must investigate Miriam's death. It is in the public's interest to ensure our government acted responsibly not only from a criminal or a civil perspective but from an internal agency perspective. It is also in the public's interest to avoid a similar tragedy in the future," she said.

But members of Congress have ignored all efforts to interest them in pursuing justice for Carey.

## 8. CONCLUSIONS

The evidence that the killing of Miriam Carey was unjust is overwhelming.

There is no question that police responded disproportionately by using deadly force against whatever threat they imagined Carey posed.

Because she never posed a threat.

All they had to do was let her go on her way.

Why did officers, instead, react so drastically?

Possible reasons:

- They were overreacting to the threat of terrorism, especially given that the Washington Navy Yard shootings, the second-deadliest mass murder on a U.S. military base, had occurred just two weeks earlier.

- They overreacted due to bad training and/or incompetence. The Secret Service has had so many serious, dangerous, and embarrassing mishaps and scandals in recent years that former agency director Julia Pierson was forced to testify at a congressional hearing in September 2014. She was then forced to resign after admitting her agency provided a false account that a White House intruder with a knife was unarmed and quickly subdued. Pierson's successor, Joe Clancy, was forced to testify before Congress in March 2015 after a pair of drunk Secret Service agents drove through the scene of an active bomb investigation at the White House.

- Miscommunication could have caused police to believe they were chasing someone actually dangerous. Even an hour after Carey was killed, when police gave their first news conference, they were still unsure if shots had been fired at the White House and were still saying she had rammed a security barrier at the White House.

- A simple lust for glory and desire to be heroes could have caused officers to shoot first and ask questions later.

- Embarrassment and ego could have caused police to over-react if they felt Carey had disrespected them by not stopping before she left the White House. Sanders suspects officers' wounded pride and a sense of retribution caused them to hunt her down.

In fact, Sanders believes a very primitive response caused Carey's death. In a soft but firm tone he insisted, "It's about male bravado.

"I'll tell you why I know that," he went on, then pointed to the picture showing the plainclothes officer confronting Carey in her car, with a cooler in one hand and the bike rack in the other. "He's in plain clothes. How is she supposed to know that he's an officer?"

Additionally, what the still pictures taken at the White House gate don't show is whether Carey tried to avoid, or go around, that officer.

Sanders thinks it is significant that investigators released only still photos, and not the surveillance video of the incident, because they "conveniently" show only what the police want seen.

"If that's the best they can do to show what this case is all about, then the public should really be afraid of these people. This is a complete cover-up."

Sanders then picked up his analysis of the photos by noting

that the plainclothes officer appears again, at the Garfield traffic circle, where shots were first fired at Carey.

Here he is at the White House:

Photo provided by U.S. Attorney.

And that appears to be him again at Garfield Circle, standing in front of the passenger-side headlight of Carey's car in the photograph on the following page.

"What the hell's he doing there?!" the attorney asked hotly, then with uncharacteristic profanity, answered his own question. He said he believed the officer chased Carey down because the one overriding thought in his mind was: "This b— f—— hit me with her car."

"I told you this was all about bravado from the beginning, didn't I?" seethed the attorney, insisting that the officer gave

Photo provided by U.S. Attorney.

chase only because he was upset at what happened at the gate, not because she had done anything illegal—because she hadn't.

Sanders said that, as a former police officer, the more he's looked at it, the more he is convinced that his first hunch was correct: that the investigation was all about officers protecting their own. "They covered up misconduct and criminal activity in this case, because what those guys did was willful."

The former officer again expressed amazement that authorities would simply announce there was insufficient evidence to press charges without showing what evidence there was to back that up.

As an example of unexplored questions, he returned to the plainclothes officer who leaned on Carey's car.

Sanders said it is "Police 101" for plainclothes officers to avoid contact because citizens may have no idea it is an officer confronting them, and that can easily cause a person to panic.

He believes that was exactly what happened to Carey, that she panicked when an unknown man, not in uniform, threw a bike rack in front of her car.

And that is why, he believes, she didn't stop.

"People get spooked. They keep saying she was mentally disturbed. There's not one shred of evidence to support that."

The problem, Sanders insisted, is the mainstream media take everything the authorities say at face value.

"For example, it says in the press release that she confronted the officers. How did she confront the officers? The officers confronted her."

Whatever ultimately caused Carey's death could have been some combination of any or all of the factors above.

And, whatever the answer is won't bring Carey back.

The bottom line: what matters most is that justice be done.

A miscarriage of justice in this case threatens the rights of us all.

What happened to Miriam Carey should concern everybody because it could happen to anybody.

Americans from Left to Right worry that the country is turning into a police state, especially with the militarization of so many local police departments with heavy war-making equipment once available only to the armed forces.

If there is no justice for Carey, it could set a disturbing precedent for local law enforcement agencies across the land.

It could exacerbate and accelerate the trend toward unaccountability by those who are supposed to defend and protect us.

If federal officers can overreact and shoot an unarmed woman in the back and kill her in plain daylight without just cause and get away with it, then every police department in the country will have received the worst possible message: some lives don't count.

Black lives don't matter. White lives don't matter. No lives matter.

Police will learn that if they make a terrible mistake and unlawfully kill someone, they will not have to pay a price, as long as they conceal the evidence. It will just go away.

But if the Carey case goes away without the truth coming to light, it will endanger everyone who still believes in a free society and the rule of law rather than the law of rulers.

Miriam Carey was just one person.

But the cover-up of her death affects us all.

# NOTES

PREFACE

1. "US Capitol Shooting: Capitol Police Hold Press Conference after Shooting," YouTube video, 2:37, posted by Big News, October 3, 2013, https://www.youtube.com/watch?v=0yFjreBKvW0.

2. United States District Court for the District of Columbia, "Police Report, Assigned October 4, 2013.

3. Metropolitan Police Department police report, http://go.wnd.com/miriamcarey/.

4. Department of Justice police report, http://go.wnd.com/miriamcarey/.


INTRODUCTION: WHY DOES THE MIRIAM CAREY STORY MATTER?

1. Garth Kant, "Legal Experts: D.C. Cops Murdered Woman," WND, December 15, 2013, http://www.wnd.com/2013/12/legal-experts-from-left-to-right-d-c-cops-murdered-woman/.

2. Ibid.

3. Michael Carl, "Who Was the Mom Who Paralyzed D.C. for a Day?" WND, February 9, 2014, http://www.wnd.com/2014/02/who-was-the-woman-who-paralyzed-d-c-for-a-day/.

4. Joseph Farah, "WND'S PULITZER PRIZE NOMINATIONS: Exclusive: Joseph Farah Explains His Obsession with Getting Justice for Miriam Carey," WND, January 29, 2016, http://www.wnd.com/2016/01/wnds-pulitzer-prize-nominations/.


CHAPTER 1: MEDIA VERSUS REALITY

1. CBS NewYork/AP, "Miriam Carey, of Stamford, Conn., Shot Dead after Capitol Hill Car Chase," October 3, 2013, CBS New York, http://newyork.cbslocal.com/2013/10/03/u-s-capitol-in-lockdown-after-report-of-shots-fired/.

2. Ashley Alman, "Miriam Carey Identified as Woman Shot by Police Near Capitol," *Huffington Post*, October 3, 2013, updated January 23, 2014, http://www.huffingtonpost.com/2013/10/03/miriam-carey-capitol-shooting_n_4040115.html.

3. Ibid.

4. Michael S. Schmidt, "Car Chase, White House to Capitol, Has Fatal End," *New York Times*, October 3, 2013, http://www.nytimes.com/2013/10/04/us/gunfire-reported-outside-the-capitol.html?_r=0.

5. David Montgomery, "How Miriam Carey's U-Turn at a White House Checkpoint Led to Her Death," *Washington Post*, November 26, 2014, http://www.washingtonpost.com/sf/style/2014/11/26/how-miriam-careys-u-turn-at-a-white-house-checkpoint-led-to-her-death/.

6. Michael O'Brien et al., "Woman Shot and Killed by Capitol Police after Chaotic Chase from White House," NBC News, October 3, 2013, http://www.nbcnews.com/news/other/woman-shot-killed-capitol-police-after-chaotic-chase-white-house-f8C11331203.

7. Jeff Zeleny, Russell Goldman, and Mike Levine, "Attempt to Ram White House Gate Ends with Conn. Woman Dead," ABC News, October 3, 2013, http://abcnews.go.com/Politics/attempt-ram-white-house-gate-ends-conn-woman/story?id=20460948.

8. Tom Cohen and Phil Gast, "Wild Car Chase Ends with Suspect Shot to Death Near U.S. Capitol," CNN, October 3, 2013, http://www.cnn.com/2013/10/03/politics/u-s-capitol-shooting-main.

9. Ibid.

10. Krissah Thompson and Scott Wilson, "Obama on Trayvon Martin: 'If I Had a Son, He'd Look Like Trayvon,'" *Washington Post*, March 23, 2012, https://www.washingtonpost.com/politics/obama-if-i-had-a-son-hed-look-like-trayvon/2012/03/23/gIQApKPpVS_story.html.

11. Michael O'Brien, "Obama: 'Trayvon Martin Could Have Been Me 35 Years Ago,'" NBC News, July 19, 2013, http://www.nbcnews.com/news/other/obama-trayvon-martin-could-have-been-me-35-years-ago-f6C10689411.

12. "Al Sharpton At Trayvon Martin Rally: 'We Are Tired Of Going To Jail For Nothing And Others Going Home For Something',", Huffington Post Black Voices, May 23, 2012, http://www.huffingtonpost.com/2012/03/23/al-sharpton-trayvon-martin-rally_n_1374975.html.

13. Rene Lynch, "Trayvon Martin Case: 'Blacks Are Under Attack,' says Jesse Jackson," *Los Angeles Times*, March 23, 2012, http://articles.latimes.com/2012/mar/23/nation/la-na-nn-trayvon-martin-case-jesse-jackson-20120323.

14. David Hudson, "President Obama Issues a Statement on the Death of Michael Brown," White House blog, August 12, 2014, https://www.whitehouse.gov/blog/2014/08/12/president-obama-issues-statement-death-michael-brown.

15. Joe Coscarelli, "Watch Al Sharpton Bring the House Down at Michael Brown's Funeral: 'This Is Not about You! This Is about Justice!'" *New York* magazine, August 25, 2014, http://nymag.com/daily/intelligencer/2014/08/al-sharpton-eulogy-michael-brown-funeral.html#.

16. David Montgomery, "Sharpton: 'Justice Will Come to Ferguson,'" *Washington Post*, November 30, 2014, https://www.washingtonpost.com/news/post-nation/wp/2014/11/30/sharpton-justice-will-come-to-ferguson/.

17. Jonathan Topaz, "Rev. Jackson: Like a 'State Execution,'" Politico, August 15, 2014, http://www.politico.com/story/2014/08/jesse-jackson-ferguson-reaction-110058.

18. Tom Hinchey, "Watch: Ben Carson Just Completely Smashed Jesse Jackson in a Debate about Ferguson," Western Journalism, August 25, 2014, http://www.westernjournalism.com/ben-carson-tells-jesse-jackson-that-michael-brown-killing-has-nothing-to-do-with-race/.

19. "The Capitol Hill Police Get Paid," YouTube video, 1:58, reposting of a C-SPAN video, posted by "pbbump," October 3, 2013, https://www.youtube.com/watch?v=dM_flkAhBNk.

20. Hannah Hess, "Capitol Police Chief Kim Dine Grilled on Miriam Carey Shooting," Roll Call, March 24, 2014, http://www.rollcall.com/news/capitol_police_chief_kim_dine_grilled_on_miriam_carey_shooting-231644-1.html.

21. United States Department of Justice, "U.S. Attorney's Office Concludes Investigation into the Death of Miriam Carey, No Charges to Be Filed in Shooting Near U.S. Capitol," July 10, 2014, https://www.google.com/?gws_rd=ssl#q=U.S.+Attorney%E2%80%99s+Office+Concludes+Investigation+into+the+Death+OF+Miriam+Carey%2C+No+Charges.

22. Montgomery, "How Miriam Carey's U-Turn at a White House Checkpoint Led to Her Death."

23. Arin Greenwood, "5 White House 'Attacks' That Didn't End in the Suspects Getting Killed," *Huffington Post*, October 4, 2013, http://www.huffingtonpost.com/2013/10/04/white-house-attacks_n_4045103.html.

24. UPI, "Man with Knife Holds Police at Bay on White House Lawn," *Sarasota Herald-Tribune*, October 4, 1978, https://news.google.com/newspapers?nid=1755&dat=19781004&id=miMhAAAAIBAJ&sjid=iGcEAAAAIBAJ&pg=2808,1603672&hl=en.

25. Eric Schmitt, "Gunman Shoots at White House from Sidewalk," *New York Times*, October 30, 1994, http://www.nytimes.com/1994/10/30/us/gunman-shoots-at-white-house-from-sidewalk.html.

26. Peter Hermann, "Ohio Man Sentenced to Prison for Launching Driverless Jeep at White House," *Washington Post*, January 10, 2014, https://www.washingtonpost.com/local/crime/ohio-man-sentenced-to-prison-for-launching-driverless-jeep-at-white-house/2014/01/10/24a843fc-7a20-11e3-8963-b4b654bcc9b2_story.html?wpisrc=nl_buzz.

27. Carol D. Leonnig, "White House Fence-Jumper Made It Far Deeper into Building Than Previously Known," *Washington Post*, September 29, 2014, https://www.washingtonpost.com/politics/white-house-fence-jumper-made-it-far-deeper-into-building-than-previously-known/2014/09/29/02efd53e-47ea-11e4-a046-120a8a855cca_story.html.

28. Chelsea J. Carter, "'My Sister Just Totally Didn't Deserve This,'" CNN, October 7, 2013, http://www.cnn.com/2013/10/04/us/dc-shooting-carey-sisters/.

29. Montgomery, "How Miriam Carey's U-Turn at a White House Checkpoint Led to Her Death."

30. Michael Carl, "Who was the mom who paralyzed D.C. for a day?" WND, February 9, 2014, http://www.wnd.com/2014/02/who-was-the-woman-who-paralyzed-d-c-for-a-day/.

31. Susan Donaldson James, "Miriam Carey: Capitol Hill Chaos Puts Postpartum Psychosis in Spotlight," ABC News, October 4, 2013, http://abcnews.go.com/Health/miriam-carey-capitol-hill-chaos-puts-postpartum-psychosis/story?id=20469977.

32. CBS NewYork/AP, "Miriam Carey, Woman Killed in Capitol Chase, Thought Obama Was 'Listening to Her,'" CBS New York, October 4, 2013, http://newyork.cbslocal.com/2013/10/04/mother-of-stamford-woman-killed-in-capitol-chase-says-daughter-was-depressed/.

33. "Miriam Carey—Police Reports," *Washington Post*, http://apps.washingtonpost.com/g/documents/local/miriam-carey-police-reports/640/.

34. Montgomery, "How Miriam Carey's U-Turn at a White House Checkpoint Led to Her Death."

35. Steve Almasy, "Woman Killed during D.C. Chase Was Shot Five Times from Behind, Autopsy Shows," CNN, April 10, 2014, http://www.cnn.com/2014/04/08/us/miriam-carey-autopsy/.

36. Ibid.

37. James Nye and Daily Mail Reporter, "Mother who rammed car into White House was shot five times in the back," Daily Mail, April 8, 2014, http://www.dailymail.co.uk/news/article-2599461/Family-mother-killed-police-ramming-White-House-barrier-demand-prosecutions-revealed-shot-FIVE-times-BACK.html.

38. Almasy, "Woman Killed during D.C. Chase Was Shot Five Times from Behind, Autopsy Shows."

39. Montgomery, "How Miriam Carey's U-Turn at a White House Checkpoint Led to Her Death."

40. Michael Carl, "Who was the mom who paralyzed D.C. for a day?" WND, February 9, 2014, http://www.wnd.com/2014/02/who-was-the-woman-who-paralyzed-d-c-for-a-day/.

41. Montgomery, "How Miriam Carey's U-Turn at a White House Checkpoint Led to Her Death."

42. Mark Steyn, "The Drift toward Despotism," *National Review*, November 8, 2013, http://www.nationalreview.com/article/363531/drift-toward-despotism-mark-steyn.

43. "World Exclusive: Obama's Secret 'Love Child' Conspiracy," *National Enquirer*, January 21, 2015, http://www.nationalenquirer.com/celebrity/world-exclusive-obamas-secret-love-child-conspiracy.

44. "Shock: Family of Woman Killed in DC Calls for Obama Paternity Test; Love Child?" RedFlag News, http://www.redflagnews.com/headlines/shock-family-of-woman-killed-in-dc-calls-for-obama-paternity-test-love-child.

45. Garth Kant, "Why did Capitol cops cut down 'innocent' woman?" WND, December 3, 2013, http://www.wnd.com/2013/12/capitol-cops-gunned-down-my-innocent-sister/.

## CHAPTER 2: POLICE VERSUS REALITY

1. Judicial Watch, "Judicial Watch Files Lawsuit on behalf of WND to Obtain Documents Regarding Fatal 2013 Shooting of Miriam Carey Outside U.S. Capitol," press release, Judicial Watch Press Room, April 15, 2015, http://www.judicialwatch.org/press-room/press-releases/judicial-watch-files-lawsuit-to-obtain-documents-regarding-fatal-2013-shooting-of-miriam-carey-outside-u-s-capitol/.

2. Michael O'Brien et al., "Woman Shot and Killed by Capitol Police after Chaotic Chase from White House," NBC News, October 3, 2013, http://www.nbcnews.com/news/other/woman-shot-killed-capitol-police-after-chaotic-chase-white-house-f8C11331203.

3. Jeff Zeleny, Russell Goldman, and Mike Levine, "Attempt to Ram White House Gate Ends with Conn. Woman Dead," ABC News, October 3, 2013, http://abcnews.go.com/Politics/attempt-ram-white-house-gate-ends-conn-woman/story?id=20460948.

4. CBS NewYork/AP, "Miriam Carey, of Stamford, Conn., Shot Dead after Capitol Hill Car Chase," CBS New York, October 3, 2013, http://newyork.cbslocal.com/2013/10/03/u-s-capitol-in-lockdown-after-report-of-shots-fired/.

5. Tom Cohen and Phil Gast, "Wild Car Chase Ends with Suspect Shot to Death Near U.S. Capitol," CNN, October 3, 2013, http://www.cnn.com/2013/10/03/politics/u-s-capitol-shooting-main/.

6. Dan Friedman et al., "Connecticut Woman Miriam Carey Suffered 'Postpartum Depression' after Having Baby before Crashing White House Gate, Mom Says," *New York Daily News*, October 4, 2013, http://www.nydailynews.com/news/national/shots-fired-u-s-capitol-report-article-1.1475378.

7. Michael S. Schmidt, "Car Chase, White House to Capitol, Has Fatal End," *New York Times*, October 3, 2013, http://www.nytimes.com/2013/10/04/us/gunfire-reported-outside-the-capitol.html?_r=0.

8. FoxNews.com, "'Mass Panic': Car Chase from White House to Capitol Ends with Suspect Dead," Fox News, October 3, 2013, http://www.foxnews.com/politics/2013/10/03/us-capitol-in-lockdown-reports-shots-fired.html.

9. O'Brien et al., "Woman Shot and Killed by Capitol Police after Chaotic Chase from White House."

10. Ibid.

11. Zeleny, Goldman, and Levine, "Attempt to Ram White House Gate Ends with Conn. Woman Dead."

12. Cohen and Gast, "Wild Car Chase Ends with Suspect Shot to Death Near U.S. Capitol."

13. FoxNews.com, "'Mass Panic': Car Chase from White House to Capitol Ends with Suspect Dead,"

14. Schmidt, "Car Chase, White House to Capitol, Has Fatal End."

15. David Montgomery, "How Miriam Carey's U-Turn at a White House Checkpoint Led to Her Death," *Washington Post*, November 26, 2014, http://www.washingtonpost.com/sf/style/2014/11/26/how-miriam-careys-u-turn-at-a-white-house-checkpoint-led-to-her-death/.

16. Department of Justice, Penn. Traffic cam video, DVD #34, 1100 Penn. Ave. NW looking East, time frame: 1400–1500 on 10/3/13, http://go.wnd.com/miriamcarey/.

17. "U.S. Attorney's Office Concludes Investigation into the Death of Miriam Carey No Charges to Be Filed in Shooting Near U.S. Capitol," United States Department of Justice, July 10, 2014, http://www.justice.gov/usao-dc/pr/us-attorney-s-office-concludes-investigation-death-miriam-careyno-charges-be-filed.

18. Hannah Hess, "Capitol Police Chief Kim Dine Grilled on Miriam Carey Shooting," Roll Call, March 24, 2014, http://www.rollcall.com/news/capitol_police_chief_kim_dine_grilled_on_miriam_carey_shooting-231644-1.html?utm_content=bufferf50ac&utm_medium=social&utm_source=facebook.com&utm_campaign=buffer.

19. Federal Law Enforcement Training Centers (FLETC) Legal Division Handbook, Homeland Security, 2015, https://www.fletc.gov/sites/default/files/2015%20Legal%20Division%20Student%20Handbook%20-%20Web%20Version%20-%20FINAL_0.pdf.

20. Schmidt, "Car Chase, White House to Capitol, Has Fatal End."

21. Ibid.

22. David Montgomery, "How Miriam Carey's U-Turn at a White House Checkpoint Led to Her Death," Washington Post, November 26, 2014, http://www.washingtonpost.com/sf/style/2014/11/26/how-miriam-careys-u-turn-at-a-white-house-checkpoint-led-to-her-death/.

23. Associated Press, "Connecticut unit a collaboration of crime-fighting skills," New Haven Register, January 4, 2014, http://www.nhregister.com/general-news/20140104/connecticut-unit-a-collaboration-of-crime-fighting-skills.

24. "Alhurra TV: Capitol Car Chase Caught on Camera," YouTube video, 1:27, posted by AFP news agency on October 3, 2013, https://www.youtube.com/watch?v=V06A5Iu_u-0.

25. Office of the Chief Medical Examiner, "Autopsy Report" for Miriam Iris Carey, October 4, 2013, Government of the District of Columbia, https://www.scribd.com/doc/216342741/The-Autopsy-Report-of-Miriam-Iris-Carey.

26. David Brown, "Could Modern Medicine Have Saved Lincoln?" Washington Post, May 21, 2007, http://www.washingtonpost.com/wp-dyn/content/article/2007/05/20/AR2007052000873.html.

27. Peter Hermann, Ed O'Keefe, and David A. Fahrenthold, "Driver Killed after Car Chase from White House to Capitol," Washington Post, October 3, 2013, https://www.washingtonpost.com/politics/police-lock-down-capitol-after-shots-fired/2013/10/03/48459e0e-2c5a-11e3-8ade-a1f23cda135e_story.html.

CHAPTER 3: MISSING EVIDENCE

1. David Montgomery, "How Miriam Carey's U-Turn at a White House Checkpoint Led to Her Death," Washington Post, November 26, 2014, http://www.washingtonpost.com/sf/style/2014/11/26/how-miriam-careys-u-turn-at-a-white-house-checkpoint-led-to-her-death/.

2.   Michael Isikoff, "Secret Service, Capitol Police radios couldn't communicate during DC chase" NBC News, October 4, 2013, http://www.nbcnews.com/news/other/secret-service-capitol-police-radios-couldnt-communicate-during-dc-chase-f8C11339861.

3.   Hannah Hess, "Interoperability Isn't Only Reason For Capitol Police Radio Upgrade," November 4, 2013, http://www.rollcall.com/news/interoperability_isnt_only_reason_for_capitol_police_radio_upgrade-228866-1.html.


## CHAPTER 4: JUSTICE DENIED

1.   The first of these articles was: Jeff Leen et al., "D.C. Police Lead Nation in Shootings," *Washington Post*, November 15, 1998, http://www.washingtonpost.com/wp-srv/local/longterm/dcpolice/deadlyforce/police1full.htm.

2.   Jeff Leen, "Objectivity Questioned in Shootings Probe," *Washington Post*, March 11, 1999, http://www.washingtonpost.com/wp-srv/local/daily/march99/holder11.htm.

3.   James Bovard, "Eric Holder's Police Shooting Record? Dismal: Column," *USA Today*, August 20, 2014, http://www.usatoday.com/story/opinion/2014/08/20/ferguson-holder-investigation-police-shooting-column/14332185/.

4.   Bovard, "Eric Holder's Police Shooting Record? Dismal: Columns."

5.   Leen, "Objectivity Questioned in Shootings Probe."

6.   Bovard, "Eric Holder's Police Shooting Record? Dismal: Columns."

7.   Ibid.

8.   Leen, "Objectivity Questioned in Shootings Probe."

9.   Ibid.

10.  Leen et al., "District Police Lead Nation in Shootings."

11.  Leen, "Objectivity Questioned in Shootings Probe."

12.  Bovard, "Eric Holder's Police Shooting Record? Dismal: Column."

13.  Jim Fisher, "Police Involved Shooting Statistics: A National One-Year Summary," *Jim Fisher True Crime* (blog), December 25, 2013.

14.  "Excerpts of Attorney General Eric Holder's Remarks at a Community College," website of the United States Department of Justice, August 20, 2014, https://www.justice.gov/opa/speech/excerpts-attorney-general-eric-holder-s-remarks-community-college.

15.  Ibid.

16.  The officers' names are redacted to protect their anonymity.

17.  Hannah Hess, "Capitol Police Ordered Not to Arrest Driver in SOTU Car Chase," *Roll Call*, January 21, 2015, http://www.rollcall.com/news/policy/capitol-police-ordered-not-to-arrest-driver-in-sotu-car-chase#sthash.dlgGsDoz.dpuf.

18.  Hannah Hess, "Driver in SOTU Police Chase Had No License, Police Say," Roll Call, January 23, 2014, http://www.rollcall.com/news/driver-in-sotu-police-chase-had-no-valid-license-police-say.

19.  Hannah Hess, "Capitol Police Chief Kim Dine Grilled on Miriam Carey Shooting," Roll Call, March 24, 2014, http://www.rollcall.com/news/capitol_police_chief_kim_dine_grilled_on_miriam_carey_shooting-231644-1.html?utm_content=bufferf50ac&utm_medium=social&utm_source=facebook.com&utm_campaign=buffer.

# INDEX

1/26/18